Career
SUCCESS

Marsha Fralick

Kendall Hunt
publishing company

D0572415

Cover image © Shutterstock, Inc.

Kendall Hunt
publishing company

www.kendallhunt.com
Send all inquiries to:
4050 Westmark Drive
Dubuque, IA 52004-1840

Copyright © 2014 by Kendall Hunt Publishing Company

ISBN 978-1-4652-3962-4

Printed in the United States of America
10 9 8 7 6 5 4 3 2

BRIEF CONTENTS

CONTENTS

PREFACE

Among the most important decisions a person will make in life are, "What is my major?" and "What is my ideal career?" I have observed that students choose their careers for a variety of reasons. Some students choose a career based on a person they admire. Maybe they have experienced a nurse who was helpful or a veterinarian that took care of a pet and based their career decisions on this personal experience. Some choose their career based on familiarity. They choose occupations that they have observed in their families or communities. Others choose a career by accident; they obtain whatever job is available. This can result in dissatisfaction and a dislike of work if the occupation is not a good match with personal strengths and interests. We now have a great deal of information on how to choose a satisfying career goal. The first step is personal assessment. What are the students' personality types, interests, skills, and values? Once these are determined, what careers match these personal characteristics?

Knowing your personal strengths and skills will help you to find your passion so that you can find personal fulfillment in the career you choose. The famous painter, Picasso, found work to be relaxing and said that time flies when you have found your passion. One of the famous quotes by author Mark Twain was, "The secret of success is making your vocation your vacation." He added that if you do this, you never have to work a day in your life. Aviator Charles Lindbergh said, "It is the greatest shot of adrenaline to be doing what you've wanted to do so badly. You almost feel like you could fly without the plane." When we find careers that match our personalities and personal strengths, we provide meaning and interest to our lives.

Over the years I have asked students to state why they are going to college and they frequently state that their goal is to be happy. However, if they do not have a clear idea of what happiness means, they may not reach their goal. Sometimes we define happiness by the things in our lives: our homes, cars, and money for vacations and other goods. Psychologist Martin Seligman, author of *Authentic Happiness*, has found that true happiness exists when you have found your passion and experience the state of "flow," when you are completely absorbed in an activity that matches your personal strengths. When you are in this state of flow, you are happier and more productive. You don't have to spend the work week looking forward to Fridays.

The greatest disappointment for a college student is to graduate from college and be unable to find a job in their chosen career. Today it is important to take a look at the job outlook and match your personal strengths to jobs that are available and pay enough for you to live your preferred lifestyle. To assure that you can find your preferred career after graduation, it is important to start the career planning process early. Determine your strengths, examine the job outlook, and prepare for your career, starting at the beginning of college rather than waiting until after graduation. It is also important to be able to use updated job search strategies to find your job. Establish your personal brand online and use new media and social networking to find a job.

After over 40 years in education, my greatest satisfaction is helping students to discover their personal strengths, interests, skills, and values and to use this knowledge to find happiness in careers that provide personal fulfillment. This is my motivation for writing *Career Success*. I hope you find it helpful.

FEATURES OF THIS BOOK

- Chapter 1, Create Your Success, helps students take responsibility for career planning and provides them with tools for motivation, positive thinking, adopting successful beliefs, and using humor to provide relaxation and perspective.

- Concepts from positive psychology are used to help students build on their strengths, think positively about the future, and clarify what happiness means to them.

- The Do What You Are (DWYA) personality assessment helps students identify their personal strengths and suggests matching careers. Supporting textbook material helps students to understand personality type and how it is connected to career choice and other success skills.

- The Interest Profiler integrated into Chapter 3 helps students identify their vocational interests. Career interest areas and matching careers are available on the O*Net database of careers.

- Material in Chapter 3 helps students clarify their values and encourages students to act on their values and use them in career decision making.

- The MI Advantage helps students identify their multiple intelligences and careers that match their highest intelligences.

- An online career portfolio summarizes the results of the DWYA and MI Advantage and provides links to the O*Net database of careers as well as links to current available jobs at Simply Hired.

- Material is provided to help students set goals based on personality type, interests, values, and multiple intelligences.

- Information is provided on current career trends, the career decision-making process, educational planning, and researching career information and outlook.

- Updated job search strategies include the concept of online personal branding and using social media and other online job search tools.

- Interactive activities within the text help students to practice the material learned.

- Frequent quizzes and answer keys within the chapters help students with reading comprehension and check their understanding of key concepts.

- Journal entries help students think critically and apply what they have learned to their personal lives.

- Individual and group exercises are included at the end of each chapter.

- The College Success Website at www.collegesuccess1.com has resources for faculty and students. Student resources include key ideas, Internet links related to each chapter, and Word documents for journal entries. Resources for faculty include the **Instructor Manual** and **Faculty Resources** for teaching college success courses, including over 500 pages of classroom exercises, handouts, video suggestions, Internet links to related material, and much more.

ACKNOWLEDGMENTS

I would like to give my sincere thanks to:

- My parents, Clarence and Betty Finley, who taught me the value of education.
- My seven brothers and sisters who taught me to laugh at life.
- My children, Mark Fralick and Sara Corbett, who challenge me to keep up to date with technology.
- Paul Delys, who provided love and encouragement and shared many of his ideas and materials for this book.
- The many instructors who tried out my materials, gave valuable feedback, and shared their ideas.
- The many students who have taken my courses over the years and shared their insights and experiences with me.

ABOUT THE AUTHOR

Dr. Marsha Fralick has been employed in the field of education for over 45 years, including 35 years teaching college and career success courses. She has brought together theories from counseling, positive psychology, and career development to provide students with strategies for career success. Her College and Career Success Program at Cuyamaca College in El Cajon, California, is recognized as an exemplary program by students and statewide organizations. In 2011 she received recognition for her lifetime of achievement by receiving an award for Outstanding First-Year Student Advocate sponsored by the National Resource Center for the First-Year Experience and Students in Transition from the University of South Carolina. Her college and career success materials are now used by community colleges and universities nationwide. She has a doctorate from the University of Southern California in higher education with an emphasis in career counseling, a master's degree in counseling from the University of Redlands, and a bachelor's degree in Spanish and English from Arizona State University. She currently resides in San Diego, California.

Create Your Success

Learning
OBJECTIVES

Read to answer these key questions:

- What are the steps in choosing a major and planning a career?

- How does education affect my future earnings?

- How can I motivate myself to be successful?

- How can I increase my positive thinking about the future?

- How can I take control of my life and create the future I want?

- How do beliefs affect my future success?

- What are some secrets to happiness?

- What does happiness mean to me?

© 2013, SHUTTERSTOCK, INC.

Most students go to college to find happiness, fulfillment, and a satisfying career. The first step is choosing a major and finding the career that matches your personal strengths, interests, and values. One of the keys to success is the belief that you can create your success and then take the steps to make it happen. In this chapter you will explore motivational techniques for increasing your success and some tools for creating the future you want. Finally, you will give some thought to what happiness means to you.

Choosing Your Major and Finding Your Ideal Career

Choosing your major is one of the most important decisions you will make in college, because it will have a big impact on your future career. It is difficult to motivate yourself and put in the work necessary to be successful if you do not have a clear picture of your future career. How do people choose a major and then find their ideal career? This course will help you to become aware of the steps needed to think critically about yourself and the world of work to make a good career decision. Here are the steps in choosing your major and finding that ideal career:

- **Realize that you can create your own future.** Chapter 1 provides some tools for creating your future, including motivation, thinking positively, understanding locus of control, optimism, belief in yourself, visualizing your success, and thinking about what it really means to be happy in your life.
- **Assess your personality type.** The Do What You Are personality assessment in Chapter 2 will help you to identify your personal strengths and matching careers. It will also give you some information about what is required for career satisfaction.
- **Explore your vocational interests and values.** The Interest Profiler integrated into Chapter 3 will help you to explore your vocational interests. Exercises within this chapter will help clarify your values, or what is most important in your life. Making a career decision based on your personal values will enable to you to find work that you find important.

- **Discover your multiple intelligences.** In Chapter 4, you will learn more about your skills by using the MI Advantage to explore your multiple intelligences and matching careers. The theory of multiple intelligences describes the many ways that people are intelligent and how they can use these skills in the workplace.
- **Learn about the job market.** Learn about career trends and opportunities in Chapter 5 and how you can match your personal strengths to the job market.
- **Gain job skills while in college.** Chapter 6 begins with some ways to increase your prospects of finding meaningful employment after college by using career services, volunteering, doing internships, and working part time.
- **Use updated job search strategies.** Chapter 6 continues with some ideas for using new media, which has provided many opportunities for marketing your personal brand and using online tools to locate your ideal job.

Journal
Entry

Write a paragraph about deciding on your ideal major and career. Use any of these questions to guide your thinking: If you have chosen a major, why is it the best major for you? Does this major help you to live your preferred lifestyle? If you have not chosen a major, what are some steps in choosing the right major and career? What qualities would you look for in an ideal career? What is your preferred lifestyle?

© 2013, SHUTTERSTOCK, INC.

> "The purpose of our lives is to give birth to the best which is within us."
> MARIANNE WILLIAMSON

Using Motivation to Increase Your Success

Education and Lifetime Earning

Many college students say that getting a satisfying job that pays well and achieving financial security are important reasons for attending college. By going to college you can get a job that pays more per hour. You can work fewer hours to earn a living and have more time for leisure activities. You can spend your time at work doing something that you like to do. A report issued by the Census Bureau in 2012 listed the following education and income statistics for all races and both genders throughout the United States.[1] Lifetime income assumes that a person works 30 years before retirement.

Average Earnings Based on Education Level

Education	Yearly Income	Lifetime Income
High School Graduate	$33,904	$1,017,120
Some College, No Degree	$37,804	$1,134,120
Associate Degree	$40,820	$1,224,600
Bachelor's Degree	$55,432	$1,662,960
Master's Degree	$67,600	$2,028,000
Professional Degree	$90,220	$2,706,600

Reprinted with special permission of North American Syndicate.

© 2013, SHUTTERSTOCK, INC.

Notice that income rises with educational level. Over a lifetime, a person with a bachelor's degree earns 66 percent more than a high school graduate. Of course these are average figures across the nation and some individuals earn higher or lower salaries. People fantasize about winning the lottery. The reality is that the probability of winning the lottery is very low. In the long run, you have a better chance of improving your financial status by going to college.

Let's do some further comparisons. A high school graduate earns an average of **$1,017,120** over a lifetime. A college graduate with a bachelor's degree earns **$1,662,960** over a lifetime. A college graduate earns **$645,840** more than a high school graduate does over a lifetime. So how much is a college degree worth? It is worth **$645,840** over a lifetime. Would you go to college if someone offered to pay you **$645,840**? Here are some more interesting figures we can derive from the table on page 4:

Completing one college course is worth **$16,146**.
(**$645,840** divided by 40 courses in a bachelor's degree)

Going to class for one hour is worth **$336**.
(**$16,146** divided by 48 hours in a semester class)

Would you take a college class if someone offered to pay you **$16,146**? Would you go to class today for one hour if someone offered to pay you **$336**? Of course, if this sounds too good to be true, remember that you will receive these "payments" over a working lifetime of 30 years.

While college graduation does not guarantee employment, it increases your chances of finding a job. In 2012 high school graduates had an unemployment rate of 12.4 percent as compared to college graduates who had an unemployment rate of 4.5 percent.[2] Increase your chances of employment by continuing your education.

Earnings and unemployment rates by educational attainment

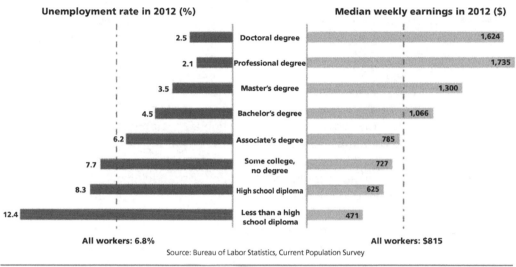

Unemployment rate in 2012 (%)		Median weekly earnings in 2012 ($)
2.5	Doctoral degree	1,624
2.1	Professional degree	1,735
3.5	Master's degree	1,300
4.5	Bachelor's degree	1,066
6.2	Associate's degree	785
7.7	Some college, no degree	727
8.3	High school diploma	625
12.4	Less than a high school diploma	471

All workers: 6.8%   **All workers: $815**

Source: Bureau of Labor Statistics, Current Population Survey

FROM HTTP://WWW.BLS.GOV/EMP/EP_CHART_001.HTM

Employment and earning are only some of the values of going to college. Can you think of other reasons to attend college? Here are some less tangible reasons.

- College helps you to develop your potential.
- College opens the door to many satisfying careers.
- College prepares you to be an informed citizen and fully participate in the democratic process.
- College increases your understanding and widens your view of the world.
- College allows you to participate in a conversation with the great minds of all times and places. For example, reading the work of Plato is like having a conversation with that famous philosopher. You can continue great conversations with your faculty and fellow students.
- College helps to increase your confidence, self-esteem, and self-respect.

Journal
Entry

What are your dreams for the future? Write a paragraph about what you hope to accomplish by going to college.

2

Intrinsic or Extrinsic Motivation

Intrinsic motivation comes from within. It means that you do an activity because you enjoy it or find personal meaning in it. With intrinsic motivation, the nature of the activity itself or the consequences of the activity motivate you. For example, let's say that I am interested in learning to play the piano. I am motivated to practice playing the piano, because I like the sound of the piano and feel very satisfied when I can play music that I enjoy. I practice because I like to practice, not because I have to practice. When I get tired or frustrated, I work through it or put it aside and come back to it, because I want to learn to play the piano well.

You can be intrinsically motivated to continue in college and achieve your career goals, because you enjoy learning and find the college experience satisfying. Look for ways to enjoy college and to find some personal satisfaction in it. If you enjoy college, it becomes easier to do the work required to be successful. Think about what you say to yourself about college. If you are saying negative things such as, "I don't want to be here," it will be difficult to continue.

Extrinsic motivation comes as a result of an external reward from someone else. Examples of extrinsic rewards are certificates, bonuses, money, praise, and recognition. Taking the piano example again, let's say that I want my child to play the piano. The child does not know if he or she would like to play the piano. I give the child a reward for practicing the piano. I could pay the child for practicing or give praise for doing a good job. There are two possible outcomes of the extrinsic reward. After a while, the child may gain skills and confidence and come to enjoy playing the piano. The extrinsic reward is no longer necessary, because the child is now intrinsically motivated. Or the child may decide that he or she does not like to play the piano. The extrinsic reward is no longer effective in motivating the child to play the piano.

You can use extrinsic rewards to motivate yourself to be successful in college. Remind yourself of the payoff for getting a college degree: earning more money, having a satisfying career, being able to purchase a car and a house. Extrinsic rewards can be a first step in motivating yourself to attend college. With experience and achievement, you may come to like going to college and may become intrinsically motivated to continue your college education.

If you use intrinsic motivation to achieve your goal, you will be happier and more successful. If you do something like playing the piano because you enjoy it, you are more likely to spend the time necessary to practice to achieve your goal. If you view college as something that you enjoy and is valuable to you, it is easier to spend the time to do the required studying. When you get tired or frustrated, tell yourself that you are doing a good job (praise yourself) and think of the positive reasons that you want to get a college education.

"Ability is what you're capable of doing. Motivation determines what you do. Attitude determines how well you do it."
RAYMOND CHANDLER

Thinking Positively about the Future

You can motivate yourself to complete your education by thinking positively about the future. If you believe that your chances of graduating from college are good, you can be motivated to take the steps necessary to achieve your goals. Conversely, if you think that your chances of graduating are poor, it is difficult to motivate yourself to continue. The degree of optimism that you possess is greatly influenced by past experiences. For example, if you were a good student in the past, you are likely to be optimistic about the future. If you struggled with your education, you may have some negative experiences that you will need to overcome. Negative thoughts can often become a self-fulfilling prophecy; what we think becomes true.

How can you train yourself to think more optimistically? First, become aware of your thought patterns. Are they mostly negative or positive? If they are negative, rewind the tape and make them more positive. Here is an example.

Pessimism

I failed the test. I guess I am just not college material. I feel really stupid. I just can't do this. College is too hard for me. My (teacher, father, mother, friend, boss) told me I would never make it. Maybe I should just drop out of college and do something else.

Optimism

I failed the test. Let's take a look at what went wrong, so I can do better next time. Did I study enough? Did I study the right material? Maybe I should take this a little slower. How can I get help so that I can understand? I plan to do better next time.

Can a person be too optimistic? In some circumstances, this is true. There is a difference between optimism and wishful thinking, for example. Wishful thinking does not include plans for accomplishing goals and can be a distraction from achieving them. Working toward unattainable goals can be exhausting and demoralizing, especially when the resources for attaining them are lacking. Goals must be realistic and achievable. Psychologists recommend that "people should be optimistic when the future can be changed by positive thinking, but not otherwise."[3] Using optimism requires some judgment about possible outcomes in the future.

There are some good reasons to think more positively. Psychologists have long-term studies showing that people who use positive thinking have many benefits over a lifetime, including good health, longevity, happiness, perseverance, improved problem solving, and enhanced ability to learn. Optimism is also related to goal achievement. If you are optimistic and believe a goal is achievable, you are more likely to take the steps necessary to accomplish the goal. If you do not believe that a goal is achievable, you are likely to give up trying to achieve it.

Being optimistic is closely related to being hopeful about the future. If you are hopeful about the future, you are likely to be more determined to reach your goals and to make plans for reaching them. One research study showed that for entering college freshmen, the level of hope was a better predictor of college grades than standardized tests or high school grade point average.[4] Students with a high level of hope set higher goals and worked to attain those goals. Hopeful people think positively and believe that the future will be good. They change goals and plans when necessary. People who are not hopeful about the future are less likely to be successful. Be optimistic about graduating from college, find the resources necessary to accomplish your goal and start taking the steps to create your success.

Activity

Are you generally an optimist or pessimist about the future? Read the following items and rate your level of agreement or disagreement.

Rate the following items using this scale:

5 I definitely agree
4 I agree
3 I neither agree or disagree (neutral)
2 I disagree
1 I strongly disagree

_____ My chances of graduating from college are good.

_____ I am confident that I can overcome any obstacles to my success.

_____ Things generally turn out well for me.

_____ I believe that positive results will eventually come from most problem situations.

_____ If I work hard enough, I will eventually achieve my goals.

_____ Although I have faced some problems in the past, the future will be better.

_____ I expect that most things will go as planned.

_____ Good things will happen to me in the future.

_____ I am generally persistent in reaching my goals.

_____ I am good at finding solutions to the problems I face in life.

Add up your total points and multiply by two. My total points (X2) are _____.

90–100	You are an excellent positive thinker.
80–89	You are a good positive thinker.
70–79	Sometimes you think positively and sometimes not. Can you re-evaluate your thinking?
60 and below	Work on positive thinking.

Journal
Entry

Write five positive statements about your college education and your future.

3

Quiz

Motivation

1. Over a lifetime a college graduate earns about _____ more than a high school graduate.
   a. $250,000
   b. $650,000
   c. $1,000,000

2. As compared to high school graduates, college graduates are
   a. more likely to be unemployed.
   b. less likely to be unemployed.
   c. guaranteed employment.

3. To be successful in college, it is best to use
   a. an external locus of control.
   b. extrinsic motivation.
   c. intrinsic motivation.

4. Intrinsic motivation
   a. comes from within.
   b. is the result of an external reward.
   c. involves higher pay or recognition for a job well done.

5. To increase your chance of accomplishing your goals,
   a. think positively and work step by step to achieve your goals.
   b. use wishful thinking.
   c. set high goals that may not be possible to achieve.

How did you do on the quiz? Check your answers: 1. b, 2. b, 3. c, 4. a, 5. a

Taking Control of Your Life

Locus of Control

Being aware of the concept of locus of control can help you take control of your life. The word **locus** means place. Locus of control is where you place the responsibility for control over your life. In other words, who is in charge? If you place the responsibility on yourself and believe that you have control over your life, you have internal locus of control. If you place the responsibility on others and think that luck or fate determines your future, you have external locus of control. Some people use internal or external locus of control in combination or favor one type in certain situations. If you favor an internal locus of control, you believe that to a great extent your actions determine your future. Studies have shown that students who use an internal locus of control are likely to have higher achievement in college.[5] The characteristics of students with internal and external locus of control are listed below.

Students with an internal locus of control:

- Believe that they are in control of their lives.
- Understand that grades are directly related to the amount of study invested.
- Are self-motivated.
- Learn from their mistakes by figuring out what went wrong and how to fix the problem.
- Think positively and try to make the best of each situation.
- Rely on themselves to find something interesting in the class and learn the material.

Students with an external locus of control:

- Believe that their lives are largely a result of luck, fate, or chance.
- Think that teachers give grades rather than students earn grades.

"I am a great believer in luck and I find that the harder I work, the more I have of it."

THOMAS JEFFERSON

- Rely on external motivation from teachers or others.
- Look for someone to blame when they make a mistake.
- Think negatively and believe they are victims of circumstance.
- Rely on the teacher to make the class interesting and to teach the material.

"Ability is what you're capable of doing.

Motivation determines what you do.

Attitude determines how well you do it."

LOU HOLTZ

© 2013, SHUTTERSTOCK, INC.

Activity

Internal or External Locus of Control

Decide whether the statement represents an internal or external locus of control and put a checkmark in the appropriate column.

Internal   External

_____ _____   1. Much of what happens to us is due to fate, chance, or luck.

_____ _____   2. Grades depend on how much work you put into them.

_____ _____   3. If I do badly on the test, it is usually because the teacher is unfair.

_____ _____   4. If I do badly on the test, it is because I didn't study or didn't understand the material.

_____ _____   5. I often get blamed for things that are not my fault.

_____ _____   6. I try to make the best of the situation.

_____ _____   7. It is impossible to get a good grade if you have a bad instructor.

_____ _____   8. I can be successful through hard work.

_____ _____   9. If the teacher is not there telling me what to do, I have a hard time doing my work.

_____ _____   10. I can motivate myself to study.

_____ _____   11. If the teacher is boring, I probably won't do well in class.

_____ _____   12. I can find something interesting about each class.

_____ _____   13. When bad things are going to happen, there is not much you can do about it.

_____ _____   14. I create my own destiny.

_____ _____   15. Teachers should motivate the students to study.

_____ _____   16. I have a lot of choice about what happens in my life.

As you probably noticed, the even-numbered statements represent internal locus of control. The odd-numbered statements represent external locus of control. Remember that students with an internal locus of control have a greater chance of success in college. It is important to see yourself as responsible for your own success and achievement and to believe that with effort you can achieve your goals.

Successful Beliefs

Stephen Covey's book, *The 7 Habits of Highly Successful People*, has been described as one of the most influential books of the 20th century.[6] In 2004 he released a new book called *The 8th Habit: From Effectiveness to Greatness*.[7] Your beliefs have a big impact on your success. Use these ideas to take control of your life and improve your chances for success.

1. **Be proactive.** Being proactive means accepting responsibility for your life. Covey uses the word "response-ability" for the ability to choose responses. The quality of your life is based on the decisions and responses that you make. Proactive people make things happen through responsibility and initiative. They do not blame circumstances or conditions for their behavior.

2. **Begin with the end in mind.** Know what is important and what you wish to accomplish in your life. To be able to do this, you will need to know your values and goals in life. You will need a clear vision of what you want your life to be and where you are headed.

3. **Put first things first.** Once you have established your goals and vision for the future, you will need to manage yourself to do what is important first. Set priorities so that you can accomplish the tasks that are important to you.

4. **Think win-win.** In human interactions, seek solutions that benefit everyone. Focus on cooperation rather than competition. If everyone feels good about the decision, there is cooperation and harmony. If one person wins and the other loses, the loser becomes angry and resentful.

5. **First seek to understand, then to be understood.** Too often in our personal communications, we try to talk first and listen later. Often we don't really listen; we use this time to think of our reply. It is best to listen and understand before speaking. Effective communication is one of the most important skills in life.

6. **Synergize.** A simple definition of synergy is that the whole is greater than the sum of its parts. If people can cooperate and have good communication, they can work together as a team to accomplish more than each individual could do separately. Synergy is also part of the creative process.

7. **Sharpen the saw.** Covey shares the story of a man who was trying to cut down a tree with a dull saw. As he struggled to cut the tree, someone suggested that he stop and sharpen the saw. The man said that he did not have time to sharpen the saw, so he continued to struggle. Covey suggests that we need to take time to stop and sharpen the saw. We need to stop working and invest some time in ourselves by staying healthy physically, mentally, spiritually, and socially. We need to take time for self-renewal.

8. **Find your voice and inspire others to find theirs.** Believe that you can make a positive difference in the world and inspire others to do the same. Covey says that leaders "deal with people in a way that will communicate to them their worth and potential so clearly that they will come to see it in themselves." Accomplishing this ideal begins with developing one's own voice or "unique personal significance."[8]

Successful Beliefs

- Be proactive
- Begin with the end in mind

- Put first things first
- Think win-win
- First seek to understand, then to be understood
- Synergize
- Sharpen the saw
- Find your voice and inspire others to find theirs

Anthony Robbins defines belief as "any guiding principle, dictum, faith, or passion that can provide meaning and direction in life. . . . Beliefs are the compass and maps that guide us toward our goals and give us the surety to know we'll get there."[9] The beliefs that we have about ourselves determine how much of our potential we will use and how successful we will be in the future. If we have positive beliefs about ourselves, we will feel confident and accomplish our goals in life. Negative beliefs get in the way of our success. Robbins reminds us that we can change our beliefs and choose new ones if necessary.

The birth of excellence begins with our awareness that our beliefs are a choice. We usually do not think of it that way, but belief can be a conscious choice. You can choose beliefs that limit you, or you can choose beliefs that support you. The trick is to choose the beliefs that are conducive to success and the results you want and to discard the ones that hold you back.[10]

© 2013, SHUTTERSTOCK, INC.

Beliefs cause us to have certain expectations about the world and ourselves. These expectations are such a powerful influence on behavior that psychologists use the term "self-fulfilling prophecy" to describe what happens when our expectations come true.

For example, if I believe that I am not good in math (my expectation), I may not try to do the assignment or may avoid taking a math class (my behavior). As a result, I am not good in math. My expectations have been fulfilled. Expectations can also have a positive effect. If I believe that I am a good student, I will take steps to enroll in college and complete my assignments. I will then become a good student. The prophecy will again come true.

Psychologist Robert Rosenthal has done some interesting research on the self-fulfilling prophecy.[11] Students in an elementary school were given an IQ test. Researchers told the teachers that this was a test that would determine "intellectual blooming." An experimental group of these students was chosen at random and teachers were told to expect remarkable gains in intellectual achievement in these children during the next eight months. At the end of this time, researchers gave the IQ test again. Students in the experimental group in which the teachers expected "intellectual blooming" actually gained higher IQ points than the control group. In addition, teachers described these students as more "interesting, curious and happy" than the control group. The teachers' expectations resulted in a self-fulfilling prophecy.

To think positively, it is necessary to recognize your negative beliefs and turn them into positive beliefs. Some negative beliefs commonly heard from college students include the following:

> *I don't have the money for college.*
> *English was never my best subject.*
> *I was never any good at math.*

When you hear yourself saying these negative thoughts, remember that these thoughts can become self-fulfilling prophecies. First of all, notice the thought. Then see if you can change the statement into a positive statement such as:

> *I can find the money for college.*
> *English has been a challenge for me in the past, but I will do better this time.*
> *I can learn to be good at math.*

If you believe that you can find money for college, you can go to the financial aid office and the scholarship office to begin your search for money to attend school. You can look for a better job or improve your money management. If you believe that you will do better in English, you will keep up with your assignments and ask the teacher for help. If you believe that you can learn to be good at math, you will attend every math class and seek tutoring when you do not understand. Your positive thoughts will help you to be successful.

> "Human beings can alter their lives by altering their attitude of mind."
> WILLIAM JAMES

Visualize Your Success

Visualization is a powerful tool for taking control of your future as well as using your brain to improve memory, deal with stress, and think positively. Coaches and athletes study sports psychology to learn how to use visualization along with physical practice to improve athletic performance. College students can use the same techniques to enhance college success.

If you are familiar with sports or are an athlete, you can probably think of times when your coach asked you to use visualization to improve your performance. In baseball, the coach reminds players to keep their eye on the ball and visualize hitting it. In swimming, the coach asks swimmers to visualize reaching their arms out to touch the edge of the pool at the end of the race. Pole-vaulters visualize clearing the pole and sometimes even go through the motions before making the jump. Using imagery lets you practice for future events and pre-experience achieving your goals. Athletes imagine winning the race or completing the perfect jump in figure skating. In this way they prepare mentally and physically and develop confidence in their abilities.

© 2013, SHUTTERSTOCK, INC.

Just as the athlete visualizes and then performs, the college student can do the same. It is said we create all things twice. First we make a mental picture and then we create the physical reality by taking action. For example, if we are building a house, we first get the idea, then we begin to design the house we want. We start with a blueprint and then build the house. The blueprint determines what kind of house we construct. The same thing happens in any project we undertake. First we have a mental picture and then we complete the project. Visualize what you would like to accomplish in your life as if you were creating a blueprint. Then take the steps to accomplish what you want.

As a college student, you might visualize yourself in your graduation robe walking across the stage to receive your diploma. You might visualize yourself in the exam room confidently taking the exam. You might see yourself on the job enjoying your future career. You can make a mental picture of what you would like your life to be and then work toward accomplishing your goal.

Journal
Entry

What tools can you use to take control of your life and create the future you want? How can you use locus of control, successful beliefs, hope, or visualization to accomplish your goals?

Secrets to Happiness

Many of you probably have happiness on your list of lifetime goals. It sounds easy, right? But what is happiness, anyway?

Psychologist Martin Seligman says that real happiness comes from identifying, cultivating, and using your personal strengths in work, love, play, and parenting."[12]

Quiz

Taking Control

1. Increase your chances of success by
   a. using external locus of control.
   b. using internal locus of control.
   c. believing that luck or fate controls your destiny.

2. The following is a statement showing internal locus of control:
   a. When bad things happen, there is not much you can do about it.
   b. Much of what happens is due to fate, chance, or luck.
   c. I can be successful through hard work.

3. Successful beliefs include the following:
   a. Put first things last.
   b. Begin with the end in mind.
   c. Think win-lose.

4. The _____ we have about ourselves determine much of our potential.
   a. beliefs
   b. doubts
   c. criticism

5. The statement, "We create all things twice," refers to
   a. doing the task twice to make sure it is done right.
   b. creating and refining.
   c. first making a mental picture and then taking action.

How did you do on the quiz? Check your answers: 1. b, 2. c, 3. b, 4. a, 5. c

You can identify these strengths by learning about your personality type, interests, and values. Seligman contrasts authentic happiness with hedonism. He states that a hedonist "wants as many good moments and as few bad moments as possible in life."[13] Hedonism is a shortcut to happiness that leaves us feeling empty. For example, we often assume that more material possessions will make us happy. However, the more material possessions we have, the greater the expectations, and we no longer appreciate what we have.

Suppose you could be hooked up to a hypothetical "experience machine" that, for the rest of your life, would stimulate your brain and give you any positive feelings you desire. Most people to whom I offer this imaginary choice refuse the machine. It is not just positive feelings we want; we want to be entitled to our positive feelings. Yet we have invented myriad shortcuts to feeling good: drugs, chocolate, loveless sex, shopping, masturbation, and television are all examples. (I am not, however, suggesting that you should drop these shortcuts altogether.) The belief that we can rely on shortcuts to happiness, joy, rapture, comfort, and ecstasy, rather than be entitled to these feelings by the exercise of personal strengths and virtues, leads to the legions of people who in the middle of great wealth are starving spiritually. Positive emotion alienated from the exercise of character leads to emptiness, to inauthenticity, to depression, and as we age, to the gnawing realization that we are fidgeting until we die.[14]

Most people assume that happiness is increased by having more money to buy that new car or HDTV. However, a process called hedonistic adaptation occurs, which makes this type of happiness short lived. Once you have purchased the new car or TV, you get used to it quickly. Soon you will start to think about a better car and a bigger TV to continue to feel happy. Seligman provides a formula for happiness:[15]

$$Happiness = S + C + V$$

"Success is getting what you want; happiness is wanting what you get."
DALE CARNEGIE

In the formula *S* stands for set range. Psychologists believe that 50 percent of happiness is determined by heredity. In other words, half of your level of happiness is determined by the genes inherited from your ancestors. In good times or bad times, people generally return to their set range of happiness. Six months after receiving a piece of good fortune such as a raise, promotion, or winning the lottery, unhappy people are still unhappy. Six months after a tragedy, naturally happy people return to being happy.

The letter *C* in the equation stands for circumstances such as money, marriage, social life, health, education, climate, race, gender, and religion. These circumstances account for 8 to 15 percent of happiness. Here is what psychologists know about how these circumstances affect happiness:

- Once basic needs are met, greater wealth does not increase happiness.
- Having a good marriage is related to increased happiness.
- Happy people are more social.
- Moderate ill health does not bring unhappiness, but severe illness does.
- Educated people are slightly happier.
- Climate, race, and gender do not affect level of happiness.
- Religious people are somewhat happier than nonreligious people.

The letter *V* in the equation stands for factors under your voluntary control. These factors account for approximately 40 percent of happiness. Factors under voluntary control include positive emotions and optimism about the future. Positive emotions include hope, faith, trust, joy, ecstasy, calm, zest, ebullience, pleasure, flow, satisfaction, contentment, fulfillment, pride, and serenity. Seligman suggests the following ideas to increase your positive emotions:

- Realize that the past does not determine your future. The future is open to new possibilities.
- Be grateful for the good events of the past and place less emphasis on the bad events.
- Build positive emotions through forgiving and forgetting.
- Work on increasing optimism and hope for the future.
- Find out what activities make you happy and engage in them. Spread these activities out over time so that you will not get tired of them.
- Take the time to savor the happy times. Make mental photographs of happy times so that you can think of them later.
- Take time to enjoy the present moment.
- Build more flow into your life. Flow is the state of gratification we feel when totally absorbed in an activity that matches our strengths.

Are you interested in taking steps to increase your happiness? Here are some activities proposed by Sonya Lyubomirsky, a leading researcher on happiness and author of *The How of Happiness*.[16] Choose the ones that seem like a natural fit for you and vary them so that they do not become routine or boring. After putting in some effort to practice these activities, they can become a habit.

1. **Express gratitude.** Expressing gratitude is a way of thinking positively and appreciating good circumstances rather than focusing on the bad ones. It is about appreciating and thanking the people who have made a positive contribution to

© 2013, SHUTTERSTOCK, INC.

your life. It is feeling grateful for the good things you have in life. Create a gratitude journal and at the end of each day write down things for which you are grateful or thankful. Regularly tell those around you how grateful you are to have them in your life. You can do this in person, by phone, in a letter, or by email. Being grateful helps us to savor positive life experiences.

2. **Cultivate optimism.** Make it a habit of looking at the bright side of life. If you think positively about the future, you are more likely to make the effort to reach your goals in life. Spend some time thinking or writing about your best possible future. Make a mental picture of your future goals as a first step toward achieving them. Thinking positively boosts your mood and promotes high morale. Most importantly, thinking positively can become a self-fulfilling prophecy. If you see your positive goals as attainable, you are more likely to work toward accomplishing them and invest the energy needed to deal with obstacles and setbacks along the way.

3. **Avoid overthinking and social comparison.** Overthinking is focusing on yourself and your problems endlessly, needlessly, and excessively. Examples of overthinking include, "Why am I so unhappy?", "Why is life so unfair?", or "Why did he/she say that?". Overthinking increases sadness, fosters biased thinking, decreases motivation, and makes it difficult to solve problems and take action to make life better.

    Social comparison is a type of overthinking. In our daily lives, we encounter people who are more intelligent, beautiful, richer, healthier, or happier. The media fosters images of people with impossibly perfect lives. Making social comparisons can lead to feelings of inferiority and loss of self-esteem.

    Notice when your are overthinking or making comparisons with others and stop doing it. Use the yell "Stop" technique to refocus your attention. This technique involves yelling "Stop" to yourself or out loud to change your thinking. Another way to stop overthinking is to distract yourself with more positive thoughts or activities. Watch a funny movie, listen to music, or arrange a social activity with a friend. If these activities are not effective, try writing down your worries in a journal. Writing helps to organize thoughts and to make sense of them. Begin to take some small steps to resolve your worries and problems.

4. **Practice acts of kindness.** Doing something kind for others increases your own personal happiness and satisfies our basic need for human connection. Opportunities

for helping others surround us each day. How about being courteous on the freeway, helping a child with homework, or helping your elderly neighbor with yard work? A simple act of kindness makes you feel good and often sets off a chain of events in which the person who receives the kindness does something kind for someone else.

5. **Increase flow activities.** Flow is defined as intense involvement in an activity so that you do not notice the passage of time. Musicians are in the flow when they are totally involved in their music. Athletes are in the flow when they are totally focused on their sport. Writers are in the flow when they are totally absorbed in writing down their ideas. The key to achieving flow is balancing skills and challenges. If your skills are not sufficient for the activity, you will become frustrated. If your skills are greater than what is demanded for the activity, you will become bored. Work often provides an opportunity to experience flow if you are in a situation in which your work activities are matched to your skills and talents.

As our skills increase, it becomes more difficult to maintain flow. We must be continually testing ourselves in ever more challenging activities to maintain flow. You can take some action to increase the flow in your life by learning to fully focus your attention on the activity you are doing. It is important to be open to new and different experiences. To maintain the flow in your life, make a commitment to lifelong learning.

6. **Savor life's joys.** Savoring is the repetitive replaying of the positive experiences in life and is one of the most important ingredients of happiness. Savoring happens in the past, present, and future. Think often about the good things that have happened in the past. Savor the present by relishing the present moment. Savor the future by anticipating and visualizing positive events or outcomes in the future.

There are many ways to savor life's joys. Replay in your mind happy days or events from the past. Create a photo album of your favorite people, places, and events and look at it often. This prolongs the happiness. Take a few minutes each day to appreciate ordinary activities such as taking a shower or walking to work. Engage the senses to notice your environment. Is it a sunny day? Take some time to look at the sky, the trees, and plants. Landscape architects incorporate art work, trees, and flowers along the freeways to help drivers to relax on the road. Notice art and objects of beauty. Be attentive to the present moment and be aware of your surroundings. Picture in your mind positive events you anticipate in the future. All of these activities will increase your "psychological bank account" of happy times and will help you deal with times that are not so happy.

7. **Commit to accomplishing your goals.** Working toward a meaningful life goal is one of the most important things that you can do to have a happy life. Goals provide structure and meaning to our lives and improve self-esteem. Working on goals provides something to look forward to in the future.

The types of goals that you pursue have an impact on your happiness. The goals that have the most potential for long-term happiness involve changing your activities rather than changing your circumstances. Examples of goals that change your circumstances are moving to the beach or buying a new stereo. These goals make you happy for a short time. Then you get used to your new circumstances and no longer feel as happy as when you made the initial change. Examples of goals that change your activities are returning to school or taking up a new sport or hobby. These activities allow you to take on new challenges that keep life interesting for a longer period of time. Choose intrinsic goals that help you to develop your competence and autonomy. These goals should match your most important values and interests.

8. **Take care of your body.** Engaging in physical activity provides many opportunities for increasing happiness. Physical activity helps to:
    *   Increase longevity and improve the quality of life.
    *   Improve sleep and protect the body from disease.
    *   Keep brains healthy and avoid cognitive impairments.
    *   Increase self-esteem.
    *   Increase the opportunity to engage in flow.
    *   Provide a distraction from worries and overthinking.

© 2013, SHUTTERSTOCK, INC.

David Myers, a professor of psychology at Hope College in Michigan, is a leading researcher on happiness. He says that 90 percent of us are naturally happy. He adds that if most of us "were characteristically unhappy, the emotional pain would lose its ability to alert us to an unusual and possibly harmful condition."[17]

Just as you have made a decision to get a college degree, make a decision to be happy. Make a decision to be happy by altering your internal outlook and choosing to change your behavior. Here are some suggestions for consciously choosing happiness.

1. Find small things that make you happy and sprinkle your life with them. A glorious sunset, a pat on the back, a well-manicured yard, an unexpected gift, a round of tennis, a favorite sandwich, a fishing line cast on a quiet lake, the wagging tail of the family dog, or your child finally taking some responsibility—these are things that will help to create a continual climate of happiness.

2. Smile and stand up straight. Michael Mercer and Maryann Troiani, authors of *Spontaneous Optimism: Proven Strategies for Health, Prosperity and Happiness*, say that "unhappy people tend to slouch, happy people don't. . . . Happy people even take bigger steps when they walk."[18]

3. Learn to think like an optimist. "Pessimists tend to complain; optimists focus on solving their problems."[19] Never use the word "try"; this word is for pessimists. Assume you will succeed.

4. Replace negative thoughts with positive ones.

5. Fill your life with things you like to do.

6. Get enough rest. If you do not get enough sleep, you will feel tired and gloomy. Sleep deprivation can lead to depression.

7. Learn from your elders. Psychologist Daniel Mroczek says that "people in their sixties and seventies who are in good health are among the happiest people in our society. . . . They may be better able to regulate their emotions, they've developed perspective, they don't get so worried about little things, and they've often achieved their goals and aren't trying to prove themselves."[20]

8. Reduce stress.

9. Take charge of your time by doing first things first.

10. Close relationships are important. Myers and Mroczek report higher levels of happiness among married men and women.[21]

11. Keep things in perspective. Will it matter in six months to a year?

12. Laugh more. Laughter produces a relaxation response.

Journal Entry

What does happiness mean to you? Write five intention statements regarding your future happiness.

5

To me happiness is . . .

I intend to . . .

© 2013, SHUTTERSTOCK, INC.

Keys to Success

Learn to Laugh at Life

"Have a laugh at life and look around you for happiness instead of sadness. Laughter has always brought me out of unhappy situations. Even in your darkest moment, you usually can find something to laugh about if you try hard enough."

RED SKELTON

© 2013, SHUTTERSTOCK, INC.

All of us face challenges in life, but if we can learn the gift of laughter and have a good sense of humor, it is easier to deal with these challenges and create the future we want to have. Laughter has important physical as well as emotional benefits. Laughter relaxes the body, boosts the immune system, and even improves the function of blood vessels and increases blood flow, which can protect the heart. It adds joy and zest to life, reduces anxiety, relieves stress, improves mood, and enhances resilience. Being more relaxed can even help you to shift perspective, solve problems, and be more creative.

Just putting a smile on your face can help. German psychologist Fritz Strack had his subjects watch a cartoon with a pencil in their mouths. Half of his subjects held the pencil between their teeth, which made them laugh. The other half of his subjects held the pencil between their lips, which made them frown. The smiling group thought that the cartoon was funnier. It seems that there is a connection between our physical responses and our internal feelings. The physical act of smiling actually makes you feel happier.[22]

If you do not feel happy, smile and pretend to feel happy. Neurophysicist Richard Hamilton says that if you pretend to be happy, you actually feel better, because positive thoughts and behavior impact the biochemistry of the brain. Positive thinking helps the brain produce seratonin, a neurotransmitter linked with feelings of happiness.[23]

Humor has several components. Humor involves looking at the incongruities of life and laughing at them. It is looking at adversity and finding the humor in the situation. It is a playful attitude and the ability to make other people smile. Most children are playful, but socialization reduces their playfulness. You can develop your sense of humor by taking yourself less seriously and being grateful for the good things in your life. Learn to laugh at yourself by shar-

ing your embarrassing moments and laughing at them. Be careful not to use humor that puts down other people or groups. Surround yourself with people who enjoy humor and laughter. Look for the humor in difficult situations. Life is full of irony and absurdity and laughing about it unites people during difficult times. By laughing at the situation, you will be in a better position to deal with it. Keep a positive perspective by focusing on the good things that are happening in your life rather than dwelling on the negatives.

The author, Mark Twain, was a good example of using humor in life. Mark Twain said that he had never worked a day in his life. He said, "What I have done I have done because it has been play. If it had been work, I shouldn't have done it." He used humor throughout his life despite facing many adversities. His father died when he was 11 years old and he started work at age 12 as a printer's apprentice. He was constantly in trouble and spent some time in jail. He served in the Civil War. His wife died at an early age and three out of four of his children died before he did.

As a child, he enjoyed playing pranks on his mother and she responded with a sense of humor. After playing a prank on his mother, she told him that he gave her more trouble than all the other children. He replied, "I suppose you were afraid I wouldn't live," and she responded, "No: afraid you would." When Mark Train almost drowned in the river, she pulled him out and said, "I guess there wasn't much danger. People born to be hanged are safe in water." Mark Twain's children described him as "a very good man and a very funny one. . . . He does tell perfectly delightful stories." He started every day by making jokes at the breakfast table and his humor is later reflected in his famous books, including *Huckleberry Finn* and *Tom Sawyer*. He wrote that "humor is a great thing . . . the saving thing after all. The minute it crops up, all our hardnesses yield, all our irritations, and resentments flit away, and a sunny spirit takes their place."[24]

The path to achieving your goals is much smoother if you choose to be happy. So relax, smile, and be happy. Then work on making positive changes in your life.

JOURNALENTRIES

CREATE YOUR SUCCESS

Go to http://www.collegesuccess1.com/JournalEntries.htm for Word files of the Journal Entries.

SUCCESS
over the Internet

Visit the *College Success Website* at http://www.collegesuccess1.com/

The *College Success Website* is continually updated with new topics and links to the material presented in this chapter. Topics include:

- Choosing a major
- Motivation
- Education and earnings
- Positive thinking
- Emotional intelligence
- Happiness

Contact your instructor if you have any problems in accessing the *College Success Website.*

Notes

1. U.S. Census Bureau, "Earnings and Unemployment by Educational Attainment 2012" available at from http://www.bls.gov/emp/ep_chart_001.htm
2. Ibid.
3. Christopher Peterson, *A Primer in Positive Psychology* (New York: Oxford University Press, 2006), 127.
4. Daniel Goleman, "Hope Emerges a Key to Success in Life," *New York Times*, December 1991, 24.
5. M. J. Findlay and H. M. Cooper, "Locus of Control and Academic Achievement: A Literature Review," *Journal of Personality and Social Psychology 44* (1983): 419–427.
6. Stephen R. Covey, *The 7 Habits of Highly Effective People* (New York: Simon and Schuster, 1989).
7. Stephen R. Covey, *The 8th Habit, from Effectiveness to Greatness* (New York: Free Press, 2004).
8. Ibid.
9. Anthony Robbins, *Unlimited Power* (New York: Fawcett Columbine, 1986), 54–55.
10. Ibid., 57.
11. Robert Rosenthal, "Self-Fulfilling Prophecy," *Psychology Today,* September 1968.
12. Martin Seligman, *Authentic Happiness, Using the New Positive Psychology to Realize Your Potential for Lasting Fulfillment.* (New York: Free Press, 2002), xiii.
13. Ibid., 6.
14. Ibid., 8.
15. Ibid., 45.
16. Sonya Lyubomirsky, *The How of Happiness* (New York: The Penguin Press, 2008).

17. Quoted in Joan Smith, "Nineteen Habits of Happy Women," *Redbook Magazine,* August 1999, 66.

18. Quoted in Smith, "Nineteen Habits of Happy Women."

19. Ibid.

20. Ibid.

21. Ibid.

22. Ibid., 68.

23. Ibid.

24. Christopher Peterson and Martin Seligman, *Character Strengths and Virtues; A Handbook and Classification* (Oxford: University Press, 2004), 583–584.

BEGIN WITH SELF-ASSESSMENT

A good way to begin this course is to assess your present skills to determine your strengths and areas that need improvement. Complete the following assessment to get an overview of the topics presented in the textbook and to measure your present skills.

© 2013, SHUTTERSTOCK, INC.

Measure Your Success

The following statements represent major topics included in the textbook. Read the following statements and rate how true they are for you at the present time. At the end of the course, you will have the opportunity to complete this assessment again to measure your progress.

5   Definitely true
4   Mostly true
3   Somewhat true
2   Seldom true
1   Never true

_____   I understand the steps in choosing a major and career.

_____   I understand how education will affect my future earnings.

_____   I know how to use motivation techniques to be successful.

_____   I have control over my life and can create my future.

_____   I usually practice positive thinking.

_____   I have a visual picture of my future success.

_____   I have a clear idea of what happiness means to me.

_____   **Total points for Creating Success**

_____   I can describe my personality type.

_____   I can list careers that match my personality type.

_____   I can describe my personal strengths and talents based on my personality type.

_____   I understand how my personality type affects how I manage my time and money.

_____   I know what college majors are most in demand.

_____   I am confident that I have chosen the best major for myself.

_____   Courses related to my major are interesting and exciting to me.

_____   **Total points for Personality and Major**

_____ I can describe my vocational interests.

_____ I can list careers that match my vocational interests.

_____ I can list my top five values.

_____ I generally consider my most important values when making decisions.

_____ My actions are generally guided by my personal values.

_____ My personal values motivate me to be successful.

_____ I can balance work, study, and leisure activities.

_____ **Total points for Interests and Values**

_____ I understand the concept of multiple intelligences.

_____ I can list my multiple intelligences.

_____ I can list my personal strengths.

_____ I can list the careers that match my personal strengths.

_____ I am aware of my emotional intelligence and use it to create positive relationships.

_____ I have a list of my short-term and long-term goals.

_____ I believe that I can create my own future.

_____ **Total points for Multiple Intelligences and Goal Setting**

_____ I understand how current employment trends will affect my future.

_____ I know what work skills will be most important for the 21st century.

_____ I know how to do career research.

_____ I am aware of the job outlook for careers in which I am interested.

_____ I have an educational plan that matches my academic and career goals.

_____ I know the steps in making a good career decision.

_____ I know how to choose a satisfying career.

_____ **Total points for Career and Education**

_____ I know how to increase my chances for employment while in college.

_____ I know how to write a good resume and cover letter.

_____ I understand personal branding and know how to market myself online.

_____ I know how to use social media to find a job.

_____ I am familiar with online tools for job search.

_____ I know how to interview for a job.

_____ I know about options for creating my own business.

_____ **Total points for Job Search Strategies**

Total your points

_____ Creating Success

_____ Personality and Major

_____ Interests and Values

_____ Multiple Intelligences and Goal Setting

_____ Career and Education

_____ Job Search Strategies

_____ **Grand total points**

If you scored

190–210   You have excellent skills for creating your future career, but you can always learn something new.

168–189   You have good skills for creating your future career, but could improve.

126–167   You have average skills for creating your future career, but will increase your skills in this course.

Below 126   Your score is low right now, but this course will help you to increase the skills for creating your future career.

What are the areas in which you scored the highest?

What areas do you need to improve?

SUCCESS WHEEL

Use your scores from "Measure Your Success" to complete the following success wheel. Use different colored markers to shade in each section of the wheel.

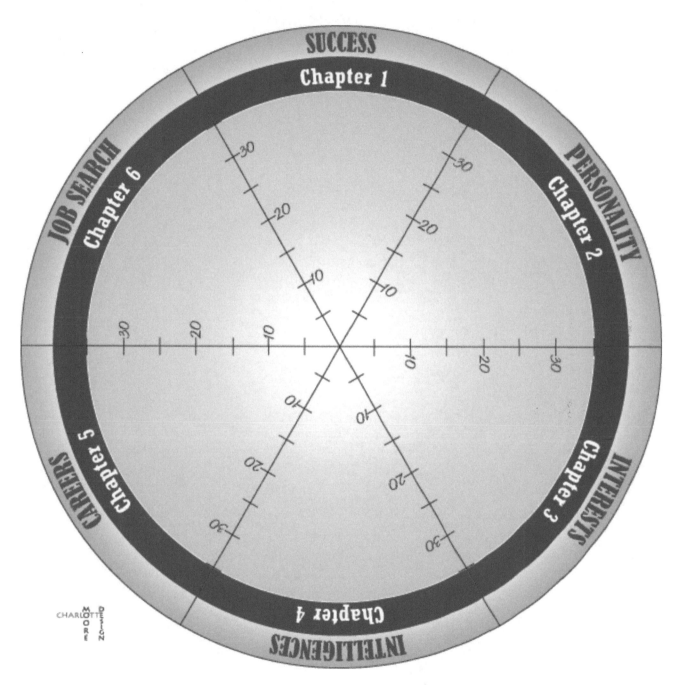

Exploring Your Personality and Major 2

Learning
OBJECTIVES

Read to answer these key questions:

- What are the different personality types?

- What is my personality type?

- What are my personal strengths?

- How is personality type related to choice of a major and career?

- What are the characteristics of my ideal career?

- What careers and majors should I consider based on my personality type?

- What are some other factors in choosing a major?

To assure your success in college, it is important to choose the major that is best for you. If you choose a major and career that match your personality, interests, aptitudes, and values, you will enjoy your studies and excel in your work. It was Picasso who said that you know you enjoy your work when you do not notice the time passing by. If you can become interested in your work and studies, you are on your way to developing passion and joy in your life. If you can get up each morning and enjoy the work that you do (at least on most days), you will surely have one of the keys to happiness.

Choose a Major That Matches Your Gifts and Talents

"To be what we are, and to become what we are capable of becoming, is the only end of life."
ROBERT LOUIS STEVENSON

The first step in choosing the major that is right for you is to understand your personality type. Psychologists have developed useful theories of personality that can help you understand how personality type relates to the choice of major and career. The personality theory used in this textbook is derived from the work of Swiss psychologist Carl Jung (1875–1961). Jung believed that we are born with a predisposition for certain personality preferences and that healthy development is based on the lifelong nurturing of inborn preferences rather than trying to change a person to become something different. Each personality type has gifts and talents that can be nurtured over a lifetime.

The theories of Carl Jung were further developed by American psychologists Katherine Briggs and her daughter Isabel Myers, who created the Myers-Briggs Type Indicator (MBTI) to measure different personality types. The connection between personality type and career choice was established through statistical analysis. The Do What You Are online personality assessment is based on the practical application of the theories of these psychologists.

While assessments are not exact predictors of your future major and career, they provide useful information that will get you started on the path of career exploration and finding the college major that is best suited to you. Knowledge of your personality and the personalities of others is not only valuable in understanding yourself, but also in appreciating how others are different. This understanding of self and others will empower you to communicate and work effectively with others. Complete the Do What You Are personality assessment that is included with this textbook before you begin this chapter. (See the inside front cover for information on accessing this assessment.)

Understanding Personality Types

Just as no two fingerprints or snowflakes are exactly alike, each person is a different and unique individual. Even with this uniqueness, however, we can make some general statements about personality. When we make generalizations, we are talking about averages. These averages can provide useful information about ourselves and other people, but it is important to remember that no individual is exactly described by the average. As you read through the following descriptions of personality types, keep in mind that we are talking about generalizations or beginning points for discussion and thoughtful analysis.

As you read through your personality description from Do What You Are and the information in this text, **focus on your personal**

strengths and talents. Building on these personal strengths has several important benefits. It increases self-esteem and self-confidence, which contribute to your success and enjoyment of life. Building on your strengths provides the energy and motivation required to put in the effort needed to accomplish any worthwhile task. The assessment also identifies some of your possible weaknesses or "blind spots." Just be aware of these blind spots so that they do not interfere with your success. Being aware of your blind spots can even be used to your advantage. For example, some personality types thrive by working with people. A career that involves much public contact is a good match for this personality type, whereas choosing a career where public contact is limited can lead to job dissatisfaction. Knowing about your personality type can help you make the right decisions to maximize your potential.

Based on the work of Carl Jung, Katherine Briggs, and Isabel Myers, personality has four dimensions:

1. Extraversion or Introversion

2. Sensing or Intuition

3. Thinking or Feeling

4. Judging or Perceiving

These dimensions of personality will be defined and examined in more depth in the sections that follow.

Extraversion or Introversion

The dimension of extraversion or introversion defines how we interact with the world and how our energy flows. In the general school population, 75 percent of students are usually extraverts and 25 percent are introverts.

Extraverts (E) focus their energy on the world outside themselves. They enjoy interaction with others and get to know a lot of different people. They enjoy and are usually good at communication. They are energized by social interaction and prefer being active. These types are often described as talkative and social.

Introverts (I) focus their energy on the world inside of themselves. They enjoy spending time alone to think about the world in order to understand it. Introverts prefer more limited social contacts, choosing smaller groups or one-on-one relationships. These types are often described as quiet or reserved.

We all use the introvert and extravert modes while functioning in our daily lives. Whether a person is an extravert or an introvert is a matter of preference, like being left- or right-handed. We can use our nondominant hand, but it is not as comfortable as using our dominant hand. We are usually more skillful in using the dominant hand. For example, introverts can learn to function well in social situations, but later may need some peace and quiet to recharge. On the other hand, social contact energizes the extravert.

One personality type is not better than the other: it is just different. Being an extravert is not better than being an introvert. Each type has unique gifts and talents that can be used in different occupations. An extravert might enjoy working in an occupation with lots of public contact, such as being a receptionist or handling public relations. An introvert might enjoy being an accountant or writer. However, as with all of the personality dimensions, a person may have traits of both types.

Activity

Introverts and Extraverts

The list below describes some qualities of introverts and extraverts. **For each pair of items**, quickly choose the phrase that describes you best and place a checkmark next to it. Remember that one type is not better than another. You may also find that you are a combination type and act like an introvert in some situations and an extravert in others. Each type has gifts and talents that can be used in choosing the best major and career for you. To get an estimate of your preference, notice which column has the most checkmarks.

Introvert (I)	Extravert (E)
_____ Energized by having quiet time alone	_____ Energized by social interaction
_____ Tend to think first and talk later	_____ Tend to talk first and think later
_____ Tend to think things through quietly	_____ Tend to think out loud
_____ Tend to respond slowly, after thinking	_____ Tend to respond quickly, before thinking
_____ Avoid being the center of attention	_____ Like to be the center of attention
_____ Difficult to get to know, private	_____ Easy to get to know, outgoing
_____ Have a few close friends	_____ Have many friends, know lots of people
_____ Prefer quiet for concentration	_____ Can read or talk with background noise
_____ Listen more than talk	_____ Talk more than listen
_____ View telephone calls as a distraction	_____ View telephone calls as a welcome break
_____ Talk to a few people at parties	_____ Talk to many different people at parties
_____ Share special occasions with one or a few people	_____ Share special occasions with large groups
_____ Prefer to study alone	_____ Prefer to study with others in a group
_____ Prefer the library to be quiet	_____ Talk with others in the library
_____ Described as quiet or reserved	_____ Described as talkative or friendly
_____ Work systematically	_____ Work through trial and error

Here are some qualities that describe the ideal work environment. Again, as you read through each pair of items, place a checkmark next to the work environment that you prefer.

Introvert (I)	Extravert (E)
_____ Work alone or with individuals	_____ Much public contact
_____ Quiet for concentration	_____ High-energy environment
_____ Communication one-on-one	_____ Present ideas to a group
_____ Work in small groups	_____ Work as part of a team
_____ Focus on one project until complete	_____ Variety and action
_____ Work without interruption	_____ Talk to others
_____ **Total** (from both charts above)	_____ **Total** (from both charts above)

Do these results agree with your personality assessment on the Do What You Are? If your results are the same, this is a good indication that your results are useful and accurate. Are there some differences with the results obtained from your personality assessment? If your results are different, this provides an opportunity for further reflection about your personality type. Here are a couple of reasons why your results may be different.

1. You may be a combination type with varying degrees of preference for each type.

2. You may have chosen your personality type on the Do What You Are based on what you think is best rather than what you truly are. Students sometimes do this because of the myth that there are good and bad personality types. It is important to remember that each personality type has strengths and weaknesses. By identifying strengths, you can build on them by choosing the right major and career. By being aware of weaknesses, you can come up with strategies to compensate for them to be successful.

Look at the total number of checkmarks for extravert and introvert on the two above charts. Do you lean toward being an introvert or an extravert? Remember that one type is not better than the other and each has unique gifts and talents. On the chart below, place an X on the line to indicate how much you prefer introversion or extraversion. If you selected most of the introvert traits, place your X somewhere on the left side. If you selected most of the extravert traits, place your X somewhere on the right side. If you are equally introverted and extraverted, place your X in the middle.

Introvert _____|_____ Extravert

Do you generally prefer introversion or extraversion? In the box below, write **I** for introversion or **E** for extraversion. If there is a tie between **E** and **I**, write **I**.

Notice that it is possible to be a combination type. At times you might prefer to act like an introvert, and at other times you might prefer to act like an extravert. It is beneficial to be able to balance these traits. However, for combination types, it is more difficult to select specific occupations that match this type

Journal Entry

Look at the results from Do What You Are and your own self-assessment above. Are you an introvert or an extravert or a combination of these two types? Can you give examples of how it affects your social life, school, or work? Write a paragraph about this preference.

Sensing or Intuition

The dimension of sensing or intuition describes how we take in information. In the general school population, 70 percent of students are usually sensing types and 30 percent are intuitive types.

Sensing (S) persons prefer to use the senses to take in information (what they see, hear, taste, touch, smell). They focus on "what is" and trust information that is concrete and observable. They learn through experience.

Intuitive (N) persons rely on instincts and focus on "what could be." While we all use our five senses to perceive the world, intuitive people are interested in relationships, possibilities, meanings, and implications. They value inspiration and trust their "sixth sense" or hunches. (Intuitive is designated as **N** so it is not confused with **I** for Introvert.)

We all use both of these modes in our daily lives, but we usually have a preference for one mode or the other. Again, there is no best preference. Each type has special skills that can be applied to the job market. For example, you would probably want your tax preparer to be a sensing type who focuses on concrete information and fills out your tax form correctly. An inventor or artist would probably be an intuitive type.

Activity

Sensing and Intuitive

Here are some qualities of sensing and intuitive persons. **As you read through each pair of items,** quickly place a checkmark next to the item that usually describes yourself.

Sensing (S)	INtuitive (N)
_____ Trust what is certain and concrete	_____ Trust inspiration and inference
_____ Prefer specific answers to questions	_____ Prefer general answers that leave room for interpretation
_____ Like new ideas if they have practical applications (if you can use them)	_____ Like new ideas for their own sake (you don't need a practical use for them)
_____ Value realism and common sense	_____ Value imagination and innovation
_____ Think about things one at a time and step by step	_____ Think about many ideas at once as they come to you
_____ Like to improve and use skills learned before	_____ Like to learn new skills and get bored using the same skills
_____ More focused on the present	_____ More focused on the future
_____ Concentrate on what you are doing	_____ Wonder what is next
_____ Do something	_____ Think about doing something
_____ See tangible results	_____ Focus on possibilities
_____ If it isn't broken, don't fix it	_____ There is always a better way to do it

Sensing (S)	INtuitive (N)
_____ Prefer working with facts and figures	_____ Prefer working with ideas and theories
_____ Focus on reality	_____ Use fantasy
_____ Seeing is believing	_____ Anything is possible
_____ Tend to be specific and literal (say what you mean)	_____ Tend to be general and figurative (use comparisons and analogies)
_____ See what is here and now	_____ See the big picture

Here are some qualities that describe the ideal work environment. Again, as you read through each pair of items, place a checkmark next to the work environment that you prefer.

Sensing (S)	INtuitive (N)
_____ Use and practice skills	_____ Learn new skills
_____ Work with known facts	_____ Explore new ideas and approaches
_____ See measurable results	_____ Work with theories
_____ Focus on practical benefits	_____ Use imagination and be original
_____ Learn through experience	_____ Freedom to follow your inspiration
_____ Pleasant environment	_____ Challenging environment
_____ Use standard procedures	_____ Invent new products and procedures
_____ Work step-by-step	_____ Work in bursts of energy
_____ Do accurate work	_____ Find creative solutions
_____ **Total** (from both charts above)	_____ **Total** (from both charts above)

Look at the two charts above and see whether you tend to be more sensing or intuitive. One preference is not better than another: it is just different. On the chart below, place an X on the line to indicate your preference for sensing or intuitive. Again, notice that it is possible to be a combination type with both sensing and intuitive preferences.

Sensing _____|_____Intuitive

Do you generally prefer sensing or intuition? In the box below, write **S** for sensing or **N** for intuitive. If there is a tie between **S** and **N**, write **N**.

☐

Journal Entry

Look at the results from Do What You Are and your own self-assessment above. Are you a sensing, intuitive, or combination type? Can you give examples of how it affects your social life, school, or work? Write a paragraph about this preference.

Thinking or Feeling

The dimension of thinking or feeling defines how we prefer to make decisions. In the general school population, 60 percent of males are thinking types and 40 percent are feeling types. For females, 60 percent are feeling types and 40 percent are thinking types.

Thinking (T) individuals make decisions based on logic. They are objective and analytical. They look at all the evidence and reach an impersonal conclusion. They are concerned with what they think is right.

Feeling (F) individuals make decisions based on what is important to them and matches their personal values. They are concerned about what they feel is right.

We all use logic and have feelings and emotions that play a part in decision making. However, the thinking person prefers to make decisions based on logic, and the feeling person prefers to make decisions according to what is important to self and others. This is one category in which men and women often differ. Most women are feeling types, and most men are logical types. When men and women are arguing, you might hear the following:

Man: "I think that . . ."

Woman: "I feel that . . ."

By understanding these differences, it is possible to improve communication and understanding. Be careful with generalizations, since 40 percent of men and women would not fit this pattern.

When thinking about careers, a thinking type would make a good judge or computer programmer. A feeling type would probably make a good social worker or kindergarten teacher.

Activity

Thinking and Feeling

The following chart shows some qualities of thinking and feeling types. **As you read through each pair of items,** quickly place a checkmark next to the items that usually describe yourself.

Thinking (T)	Feeling (F)
_____ Apply impersonal analysis to problems	_____ Consider the effect on others
_____ Value logic and justice	_____ Value empathy and harmony
_____ Fairness is important	_____ There are exceptions to every rule
_____ Truth is more important than tact	_____ Tact is more important than truth
_____ Motivated by achievement and accomplishment	_____ Motivated by being appreciated by others
_____ Feelings are valid if they are logical or not	_____ Feelings are valid whether they make sense
_____ Good decisions are logical	_____ Good decisions take others' feelings into account

Thinking (T)	Feeling (F)
_____ Described as cool, calm, and objective	_____ Described as caring and emotional
_____ Love can be analyzed	_____ Love cannot be analyzed
_____ Firm-minded	_____ Gentle-hearted
_____ More important to be right	_____ More important to be liked
_____ Remember numbers and figures	_____ Remember faces and names
_____ Prefer clarity	_____ Prefer harmony
_____ Find flaws and critique	_____ Look for the good and compliment
_____ Prefer firmness	_____ Prefer persuasion

Here are some qualities that describe the ideal work environment. As you read through each pair of items, place a checkmark next to the items that usually describe the work environment that you prefer.

Thinking (T)

_____   Maintain business environment

_____   Work with people I respect

_____   Be treated fairly

_____   Fair evaluations

_____   Solve problems

_____   Challenging work

_____   Use logic and analysis

_____   **Total** (from both charts above)

Feeling (F)

_____   Maintain close personal relationships

_____   Work in a friendly, relaxed environment

_____   Be able to express personal values

_____   Appreciation for good work

_____   Make a personal contribution

_____   Harmonious work situation

_____   Help others

_____   **Total** (from both charts above)

While we all use thinking and feeling, what is your preferred type? Look at the charts above and notice whether you are more the thinking or feeling type. One is not better than the other. On the chart below, place an X on the line to indicate how much you prefer thinking or feeling.

Thinking_____|_____Feeling

Do you generally prefer thinking or feeling? In the box below, write **T** for thinking or **F** for feeling. If there is a tie between **T** and **F**, write **F**.

Journal Entry

Look at the results from Do What You Are and your own self-assessment above. Are you a thinking, feeling, or combination type? Can you give examples of how it affects your social life, school, or work? Write a paragraph about this preference.

Judging or Perceiving

The dimension of judging or perceiving refers to how we deal with the external world. In other words, do we prefer the world to be structured or unstructured? In the general school population, the percentage of each of these types is approximately equal.

*Judging (J) types like to live in a structured, orderly, and planned way. They are happy when their lives are structured and matters are settled. They like to have control over their lives. **Judging does not mean to judge others.** Think of this type as being orderly and organized.*

*Perceptive (P) types like to live in a spontaneous and flexible way. They are happy when their lives are open to possibilities. They try to understand life rather than control it. **Think of this type as spontaneous and flexible.***

Since these types have very opposite ways of looking at the world, there is a great deal of potential for conflict between them unless there is an appreciation for the gifts and talents of both. In any situation, we can benefit from people who represent these very different points of view. For example, in a business situation, the judging type would be good at managing the money, while the perceptive type would be good at helping the business to adapt to a changing marketplace. It is good to be open to all the possibilities and to be flexible, as well as to have some structure and organization.

Activity

Judging and Perceptive

As you read through each pair of items, quickly place a checkmark next to the items that generally describe yourself.

Judging (J)	Perceptive (P)
_____ Happy when the decisions are made and finished	_____ Happy when the options are left open; something better may come along
_____ Work first, play later	_____ Play first, do the work later
_____ It is important to be on time	_____ Time is relative
_____ Time flies	_____ Time is elastic
_____ Feel comfortable with routine	_____ Dislike routine
_____ Generally keep things in order	_____ Prefer creative disorder
_____ Set goals and work toward them	_____ Change goals as new opportunities arise
_____ Emphasize completing the task	_____ Emphasize how the task is done
_____ Like to finish projects	_____ Like to start projects
_____ Meet deadlines	_____ What deadline?
_____ Like to know what I am getting into	_____ Like new possibilities and situations
_____ Relax when things are organized	_____ Relax when necessary
_____ Follow a routine	_____ Explore the unknown
_____ Focused	_____ Easily distracted
_____ Work steadily	_____ Work in spurts of energy

Here are some qualities that describe the ideal work environment. Again, as you **read through each pair of items**, place a checkmark next to the work environment that you prefer.

Judging (J)	**Perceptive (P)**
_____ Follow a schedule	_____ Be spontaneous
_____ Clear directions	_____ Minimal rules and structure
_____ Organized work	_____ Flexibility
_____ Logical order	_____ Many changes
_____ Control my job	_____ Respond to emergencies
_____ Stability and security	_____ Take risks and be adventurous
_____ Work on one project until done	_____ Juggle many projects
_____ Steady work	_____ Variety and action
_____ Satisfying work	_____ Fun and excitement
_____ Like having high responsibility	_____ Like having interesting work
_____ Accomplish goals on time	_____ Work at my own pace
_____ Clear and concrete assignments	_____ Minimal supervision
_____ **Total** (from both charts above)	_____ **Total** (from both charts above)

Look at the charts above and notice whether you are more the judging type (orderly and organized) or the perceptive type (spontaneous and flexible). We need the qualities of both types to be successful and deal with the rapid changes in today's world. On the chart below, place an X on the line to indicate how much you prefer judging or perceiving.

Judging _____|_____Perceptive

Do you generally have judging or perceptive traits? In the box below, write **J** for judging or **P** for perceptive. If there is a tie between **J** and **P**, write **P**.

☐

Journal Entry

Look at the results from Do What You Are and your own self-assessment above. Are you a judging, perceptive, or combination type? Can you give examples of how it affects your social life, school, or work? Write a paragraph about this preference.

"Knowing thyself is the height of wisdom."
SOCRATES

Activity

Summarize Your Results

Look at your results above and summarize them on this composite chart. Notice that we are all unique, according to where the Xs fall on the scale.

Extravert (E) _____|_____ Introvert (I)

Sensing (S) _____|_____ Intuitive (N)

Thinking (T) _____|_____ Feeling (F)

Judging (J) _____|_____ Perceptive (P)

Write the letters representing each of your preferences.

The above letters represent your estimated personality type based on your understanding and knowledge of self. It is a good idea to confirm that this type is correct for you by completing the online personality assessment, Do What You Are.

Quiz

Personality Types

Test what you have learned by selecting the correct answer to the following questions.

1. A person who is energized by social interaction is a/an:
   a. introvert
   b. extravert
   c. feeling type

2. A person who is quiet and reserved is a/an:
   a. introvert
   b. extravert
   c. perceptive type

3. A person who relies on experience and trusts information that is concrete and observable is a/an:
   a. judging type
   b. sensing type
   c. perceptive type

4. A person who focuses on "what could be" is a/an:
   a. perceptive type
   b. thinking type
   c. intuitive type

5. A person who makes decisions based on logic is a/an:
   a. thinker
   b. perceiver
   c. sensor

6. A person who makes decisions based on personal values is a/an:
   a. feeling type
   b. thinking type
   c. judging type

7. The perceptive type:
   a. has extrasensory perception
   b. likes to live life in a spontaneous and flexible way
   c. always considers feelings before making a decision

8. The judging type likes to:
   a. judge others
   b. use logic
   c. live in a structured and orderly way

9. Personality assessments are an exact predictor of your best major and career.
   a. true
   b. false

10. Some personality types are better than others.
    a. true
    b. false

How did you do on the quiz? Check your answers: 1. b, 2. a, 3. b, 4. c, 5. a, 6. a, 7. b, 8. c, 9. b, 10. b

Personality and Preferred Work Environment

Knowing your personality type will help you to understand your preferred work environment and provide some insights into selecting the major and career that you would enjoy. Selecting the work environment that matches your personal preferences helps you to be energized on the job and to minimize stress. Understanding other types will help you to work effectively with co-workers. As you read this section, think about your ideal work environment and how others are different.

Extraverts are career generalists who use their skills in a variety of ways. They like variety and action in a work environment that provides the opportunity for social interaction. Extraverts communicate well and meet people easily. They like to talk while working and are interested in other people and what they are doing. They enjoy variety on the job and like to perform their work in different settings. They learn new tasks by talking with others and trying out new ideas. Extraverts are energized by working as part of a team, leading others in achieving goals, and having opportunities to communicate with others.

Introverts are career specialists who develop in-depth skills. The introvert likes quiet for concentration and likes to focus on a work task until it is completed. They need time to think before taking action. This type often chooses to work alone or with one other person and prefers written communication such as emails to oral communication or presentations. They learn new tasks by reading and reflecting and using mental practice. Introverts are energized when they can work in a quiet environment with few interruptions. They are stressed when they have to work in a noisy environment and do not have time alone to concentrate on a project.

The **sensing** type is realistic and practical and likes to develop standard ways of doing the job and following a routine. They are observant and interested in facts and finding the truth. They keep accurate track of details, make lists, and are good at doing precise work. This type learns from personal experience and the experience of others. They use their experience to move up the job ladder. Sensing types are energized when they are doing practical work with tangible outcomes where they are required to organize facts and details, use common sense, and focus on one project at a time. They are stressed when they have to deal with frequent or unexpected change.

The **intuitive** type likes to work on challenging and complex problems where they can follow their inspirations to find creative solutions. They like change and finding new ways of doing work. This type focuses on the whole picture rather than the details. The intuitive type is an initiator, promoter, and inventor of ideas. They enjoy learning a new skill more than using it. They often change careers to follow their creative inspirations. Intuitive types are energized by working in an environment where they can use creative insight, imagination, originality, and individual initiative. They are stressed when they have to deal with too many details or have little opportunity for creativity.

The **thinking** type likes to use logical analysis in making decisions. They are objective and rational and treat others fairly. They want logical reasons before accepting any new ideas. They follow policy and are often firm-minded and critical, especially when dealing with illogic in others. They easily learn facts, theories, and principles. They are interested in careers with money, prestige, or influence. Thinking types are energized when they are respected for their expertise and recognized for a job well done. They enjoy working with others who are competent and efficient. They become stressed when they work with people they consider to be illogical, unfair, incompetent, or overly emotional.

The **feeling** type likes harmony and the support of co-workers. They are personal, enjoy warm relationships, and relate well to most people. Feeling types know their personal values and apply them consistently. They enjoy doing work that provides a service to people and often do work that requires them to understand and analyze their own emotions and those of others. They prefer a friendly work environment and like to learn with others. They enjoy careers in which they can make a contribution to humanity. Feeling types are energized by working in a friendly, congenial, and supportive work environment. They are stressed when there is conflict in the work environment, especially when working with controlling or demanding people.

The **judging** type likes a work environment that is structured, settled, and organized. They prefer work assignments that are clear and definite. The judging type makes lists and plans to get the job done on time. They make quick decisions and like to have the work finished. They are good at doing purposeful and exacting work. They prefer to learn only the essentials that are necessary to do the job. This type carefully plans their career path. Judging types are energized by working in a predictable and orderly environment with clear responsibilities and deadlines. They become stressed when the work environment becomes disorganized or unpredictable.

The **perceptive** type likes to be spontaneous and go with the flow. They are comfortable in handling the unplanned or unexpected in the work environment. They prefer to be flexible in their work and feel restricted by structures and schedules. They are good at handling work which requires change and adaptation. They are tolerant and have a "live and let live" attitude toward others. Decisions are often postponed because this type wants to know all there is to know and explore all the options before making a decision. This type is often a career changer who takes advantage of new job openings and opportunities for change. Perceptive types are energized when the work environment is flexible and they can relax and control their own time. They are stressed when they have to meet deadlines or work under excessive rules and regulations.

> "True greatness is starting where you are, using what you have, and doing what you can."
>
> ARTHUR ASHE

Personality and Decision Making

Your personality type affects how you think and how you make decisions. Knowing your decision-making style will help you make good decisions about your career and personal life as well as work with others in creative problem solving. Each personality type views the decision-making process in a different way. Ideally, a variety of types would be involved in making a decision so that the strengths of each type could be utilized. As you read through the following descriptions, think about your personality type and how you make decisions as well as how others are different.

The **introvert** thinks up ideas and reflects on the problem before acting. The **extravert** acts as the communicator in the decision-making process. Once the decision is made, they take action and implement the decision. The **intuitive** type develops theories and uses intuition to come up with ingenious solutions to the problem. The **sensing** type applies personal experience to the decision-making process and focuses on solutions that are practical and realistic.

The thinking and feeling dimensions of personality are the most important factors in determining how a decision is made. Of course, people use both thinking and feeling in the decision-making process, but tend to prefer or trust either thinking or feeling. Those who prefer **thinking** use cause-and-effect reasoning and solve problems with logic. They use objective and impersonal criteria and include all the consequences of alternative solutions in the decision-making process. They are interested in finding out what is true and what is false. They use laws and principles to treat everyone fairly. Once a decision is made, they are firm-minded, since the decision was based on logic. This type is often critical of those who do not use logic in the decision-making process. The **feeling** type considers human values and motives in the decision-making process (whether they are logical or not) and values harmony and maintaining good relationships. They consider carefully how much they care about each of the alternatives and how they will affect other people. They are interested in making a decision that is agreeable to all parties. Feeling types are tactful and skillful in dealing with people.

It is often asked if thinking types have feelings. They do have feelings, but use them as a criterion to be factored into the decision-making process. Thinking types are more comfortable when feelings are controlled and often think that feeling types are too emotional. Thinking types may have difficulties when they apply logic in a situation where a feeling response is needed, such as in dealing with a spouse. Thinking types need to know that people are important in making decisions. Feeling types need to know that behavior will have logical consequences and that they may need to keep emotions more controlled to work effectively with thinking types.

Judging and **perceptive** types have opposite decision-making strategies. The judging type is very methodical and cautious in making decisions. Once they have gone through the decision-making steps, they like to make decisions quickly so that they can have closure and finish the project. The perceptive type is an adventurer who wants to look at all the possibilities before making a decision. They are open-minded and curious and often resist closure to look at more options.

If a combination of types collaborates on a decision, it is more likely that the decision will be a good one that takes into account creative possibilities, practicality, logical consequences, and human values.

Personality and Time Management

How we manage our time is not just a result of personal habits: it is also a reflection of our personality type. Probably the dimension of personality type most connected to time management is the judging or perceptive trait. **Judging** types like to have things under control and live in a planned and orderly manner. **Perceptive** types prefer more spontaneity and flexibility. Understanding the differences between these two types will help you to better understand yourself and others.

Judging types are naturally good at time management. They often use schedules as a tool for time management and organization. Judging types plan their time and work steadily to accomplish goals. They are good at meeting deadlines and often put off relaxation, recreation, and fun. They relax after projects are completed. If they have too many projects, they find it difficult to find time for recreation. Since judging types like to have projects under control, there is a danger that projects will be completed too quickly and that quality will suffer. Judging types may need to slow down and take the time to do quality work. They may also need to make relaxation and recreation a priority.

Perceptive types are more open-ended and prefer to be spontaneous. They take time to relax, have fun, and participate in recreation. In working on a project, perceptive types want to brainstorm all the possibilities and are not too concerned about finishing projects. This type procrastinates when the time comes to make a final decision and finish a project. There is always more information to gather and more possibilities to explore. Perceptive types are easily distracted and may move from project to project. They may have several jobs going at once. These types need to try to focus on a few projects at a time in order to complete them. Perceptive types need to work on becoming more organized so that projects can be completed on time.

Research has shown that students who are judging types are more likely to have a higher grade point average in the first semester.[1] It has also been found that the greater the preference for intuition, introversion, and judgment, the better the grade point average.[2] Why is this true? Many college professors are intuitive types that use intuition and creative ideas. The college environment requires quiet time for reading and studying, which is one of the preferences of introverts. Academic environments require structure, organization, and completion of assignments. To be successful in an academic environment requires adaptation by some personality types. Extroverts need to spend more quiet time reading and studying. Sensing types need to gain an understanding of intuitive types. Perceptive types need to use organization to complete assignments on time.

Personality and Money

Does your personality type affect how you deal with money? Otto Kroeger and Janet Thuesen make some interesting observations about how different personality types deal with money.

- **Judging types (orderly and organized).** These types excel at financial planning and money management. They file their tax forms early and pay their bills on time.
- **Perceptive types (spontaneous and flexible).** These types adapt to change and are more creative. Perceivers, especially intuitive perceivers, tend to freak out as the April 15 tax deadline approaches and as bills become due.
- **Feeling types (make decisions based on feelings).** These types are not very money-conscious. They believe that money should be used to serve humanity. They are often attracted to low-paying jobs that serve others.[3]

In studying stockbrokers, these same authors note that ISTJs (introvert, sensing, thinking, and judging types) are the most conservative investors, earning a small but reliable return on investments. The ESTPs (extravert, sensing, thinking, perceptive types) and ENTPs (extravert, intuitive, thinking, perceptive types) take the biggest risks and earn the greatest returns.[4]

Journal Entry

Write a paragraph about how being a judging, perceptive, or combination type influences any of the following: how you manage your time, how you budget your money, or your preferred work environment. Remember that judging means orderly and organized, not judging other people; perceptive means spontaneous and flexible. How is this information useful in choosing your career or being successful in college?

5

Personality and Career Choice

While it is not possible to predict exactly your career and college major by knowing your personality type, it can be helpful in providing opportunities for exploration. Here are some general descriptions of personality types and preferred careers. Included are general occupational fields, frequently chosen occupations, and suggested majors. These suggestions about career selections are based on the general characteristics of each type and research that correlates personality type with choice of a satisfying career.[5] Read the descriptions, careers, and majors that match your personality type, and then continue your career exploration with the online database in the Do What You Are personality assessment included with your textbook.

> "Choose a job you love, and you will never have to work a day in your life."
>
> CONFUCIUS

© 2013, SHUTTERSTOCK, INC.

ISTJ

ISTJs are responsible, loyal, stable, practical, down-to-earth, hardworking, and reliable. They can be depended upon to follow through with tasks. They value tradition, family, and security. They are natural leaders who prefer to work alone, but can adapt to working with teams if needed. They like to be independent and have time to think things through. They are able to remember and use concrete facts and information. They make decisions by applying logic and rational thinking. They appreciate structured and orderly environments and deliver products and services in an efficient and orderly way.

General occupations to consider

business	education	health care
service	technical	military
law and law enforcement	engineering	management

Specific job titles

business executive	lawyer	electronic technician
administrator	judge	computer occupations
manager	police officer	dentist
real estate agent	detective	pharmacist
accountant	corrections officer	primary care physician
bank employee	teacher (math, trade,	nursing administrator
stockbroker	technical)	respiratory therapist
auditor	educational administrator	physical therapist
hairdresser	coach	optometrist
cosmetologist	engineer	chemist
legal secretary	electrician	military officer or enlistee

College majors

business	engineering	chemistry
education	computers	biology
mathematics	health occupations	vocational training
law		

ISTP

ISTPs are independent, practical, and easygoing. They prefer to work individually and frequently like to work outdoors. These types like working with objects and often are good at working with their hands and mastering tools. They are interested in how and why things work and are able to apply technical knowledge to solving practical problems. Their logical thinking makes them good troubleshooters and problem solvers. They enjoy variety, new experiences, and taking risks. They prefer environments with little structure and have a talent for managing crises. The ISTP is happy with occupations that involve challenge, change, and variety.

General occupations to consider

sales	technical	business and finance
service	health care	vocational training
corrections		

Specific job titles

sales manager	engineer	office manager
insurance agent	electronics technician	small business manager
cook	software developer	banker
firefighter	computer programmer	economist
pilot	radiologic technician	legal secretary
race car driver	exercise physiologist	paralegal
police officer	coach	computer repair
corrections officer	athlete	airline mechanic
judge	dental assistant/hygienist	carpenter
attorney	physician	construction worker
intelligence agent	optometrist	farmer
detective	physical therapist	military officer or enlistee

College majors

business	computers	health occupations
vocational training	biology	physical education
law		

ISFJ

ISFJs are quiet, friendly, responsible, hardworking, productive, devoted, accurate, thorough, and careful. They value security, stability, and harmony. They like to focus on one person or project at a time. ISFJs prefer to work with individuals and are very skillful in understanding people and their needs. They often provide service to others in a very structured way. They are careful observers, remember facts, and work on projects requiring accuracy and attention to detail. They have a sense of space and function that leads to artistic endeavors such as interior decorating or landscaping. ISFJs are most comfortable working in environments that are orderly, structured, and traditional. While they often work quietly behind the scenes, they like their contributions to be recognized and appreciated.

General occupations to consider

health care	education	artistic
social service	business	religious occupations
corrections	technical	vocational training

Specific job titles

nurse	social worker	counselor
physician	social services	secretary
medical technologist	administrator	cashier
dental hygienist	child care worker	accountant
health education	speech pathologist	personnel administrator
practitioner	librarian	credit counselor
dietician	curator	business manager
physical therapist	genealogist	paralegal
nursing educator	corrections worker	computer occupations
health administrator	probation officer	engineer
medical secretary	teacher (preschool,	interior decorator
dentist	grades 1–12)	home economist
medical assistant	guidance counselor	religious educator
optometrist	educational administrator	clergy
occupational therapist		

College majors

health occupations	education	graphics
biology	business	religious studies
psychology	engineering	vocational training
sociology	art	

ISFP

ISFPs are quiet, reserved, trusting, loyal, committed, sensitive, kind, creative, and artistic. They have an appreciation for life and value serenity and aesthetic beauty. These types are individualistic and generally have no desire to lead or follow; they prefer to work independently. They have a keen awareness of their environment and often have a special bond with children and animals. ISFPs are service-oriented and like to help others. They like to be original and unconventional. They dislike rules and structure and need space and freedom to do things in their own way.

General occupations to consider

artists	technical	business
health care	service	vocational training

Specific job titles

artist	recreation services	forester
designer	physical therapist	botanist
fashion designer	radiologic technician	geologist
jeweler	medical assistant	mechanic
gardener	dental assistant/hygienist	marine biologist
potter	veterinary assistant	teacher (science, art)
painter	veterinarian	police officer
dancer	animal groomer/trainer	beautician
landscape designer	dietician	merchandise planner
carpenter	optician/optometrist	stock clerk
electrician	exercise physiologist	store keeper
engineer	occupational therapist	counselor
chef	art therapist	social worker
nurse	pharmacy technician	legal secretary
counselor	respiratory therapist	paralegal

College majors

art	forestry	psychology
health occupations	geology	counseling
engineering	education	social work
physical education	business	vocational training
biology		

INFJ

INFJs are idealistic, complex, compassionate, authentic, creative, and visionary. They have strong value systems and search for meaning and purpose to life. Because of their strong value systems, INFJs are natural leaders or at least follow those with similar ideas. They intuitively understand people and ideas and come up with new ideas to provide service to others. These types like to organize their time and be in control of their work.

General occupations to consider

counseling	religious occupations	health care
education	creative occupations	social services
science	arts	business

Specific job titles

career counselor	director of religious	dental hygienist
psychologist	education	speech pathologist
teacher (high school or	fine artist	nursing educator
college English, art,	playwright	medical secretary
music, social sciences,	novelist	pharmacist
drama, foreign	poet	occupational therapist
languages, health)	designer	human resources
librarian	architect	manager
home economist	art director	marketer

social worker	health care administrator	employee assistance
clergy	physician	program
	biologist	merchandise planner
		environmental lawyer

College majors

psychology	drama	architecture
counseling	foreign languages	biology
education	English	business
art	health occupations	law
music	social work	science

INFP

INFPs are loyal, devoted, sensitive, creative, inspirational, flexible, easygoing, complex, and authentic. They are original and individualistic and prefer to work alone or with other caring and supportive individuals. These types are service-oriented and interested in personal growth. They develop deep relationships because they understand people and are genuinely interested in them. They dislike dealing with details and routine work. They prefer a flexible working environment with a minimum of rules and regulations.

General occupations to consider

creative arts	counseling	health care
education	religious occupations	organizational
		development

Specific job titles

artist	photographer	dietician
designer	carpenter	psychiatrist
writer	teacher (art, drama,	physical therapist
journalist	music, English, foreign	occupational therapist
entertainer	languages)	speech pathologist
architect	psychologist	laboratory technologist
actor	counselor	public health nurse
editor	social worker	dental hygienist
reporter	librarian	physician
journalist	clergy	human resources
musician	religious educator	specialist
graphic designer	missionary	social scientist
art director	church worker	consultant

College majors

art	foreign languages	medicine
music	architecture	health occupations
graphic design	education	social work
journalism	religious studies	counseling
English	psychology	business

INTJ

INTJs are reserved, detached, analytical, logical, rational, original, independent, creative, ingenious, innovative, and resourceful. They prefer to work alone and work best alone. They can work with others if their ideas and competence are respected. They value knowledge and efficiency. They enjoy creative and intellectual challenges and understand complex theories. They create order and structure. They prefer to work with autonomy and control over their work. They dislike factual and routine kinds of work.

General occupations to consider

business and finance	education	law
technical occupations	health care and medicine	creative occupations
science	architecture	engineering

Specific job titles

management consultant	astronomer	dentist
human resources planner	computer programmer	biomedical engineer
economist	biomedical researcher	attorney
international banker	software developer	manager
financial planner	network integration	judge
investment banker	specialist	electrical engineer
scientist	teacher (university)	writer
scientific researcher	school principal	journalist
chemist	mathematician	artist
biologist	psychiatrist	inventor
computer systems analyst	psychologist	architect
electronic technician	neurologist	actor
design engineer	physician	musician
architect		

College majors

business	physics	journalism
finance	education	art
chemistry	mathematics	architecture
biology	medicine	drama
computers	psychology	music
engineering	law	vocational training
astronomy	English	

INTP

INTPs are logical, analytical, independent, original, creative, and insightful. They are often brilliant and ingenious. They work best alone and need quiet time to concentrate. They focus their attention on ideas and are frequently detached from other people. They love theory and abstract ideas and value knowledge and competency. INTPs are creative thinkers who are not too interested in practical application. They dislike detail and routine and need freedom to develop, analyze, and critique new ideas. These types maintain high standards in their work.

General occupations to consider

planning and development	technical professional	academic creative occupations
health care		

Specific job titles

computer software designer	pharmacist	historian
computer programmer	engineer	philosopher
research and development	electrician	college teacher
systems analyst	dentist	researcher
financial planner	veterinarian	logician
investment banker	lawyer	photographer
physicist	economist	creative writer
plastic surgeon	psychologist	artist
psychiatrist	architect	actor
chemist	psychiatrist	entertainer
biologist	mathematician	musician
pharmaceutical researcher	archaeologist	inventor

College majors

computers	philosophy	mathematics
business	music	archaeology
physics	art	history
chemistry	drama	English
biology	engineering	drama
astronomy	psychology	music
medicine	architecture	vocational training

ESTP

ESTPs have great people skills and are action-oriented, fun, flexible, adaptable, and resourceful. They enjoy new experiences and dealing with people. They remember facts easily and have excellent powers of observation that they use to analyze other people. They are good problem solvers and can react quickly in an emergency. They like adventure and risk and are alert to new opportunities. They start new projects but do not necessarily follow through to completion. They prefer environments without too many rules and restrictions.

General occupations to consider

sales	entertainment	technical
service	sports	trade
active careers	health care	business
finance		

Specific job titles

marketing professional	insurance agent	dentist
firefighter	sportscaster	carpenter

police officer	news reporter	farmer
corrections officer	journalist	construction worker
paramedic	tour agent	electrician
detective	dancer	teacher (trade, industrial, technical)
pilot	bartender	
investigator	auctioneer	chef
real estate agent	professional athlete or coach	engineer
exercise physiologist		surveyor
flight attendant	fitness instructor	radiologic technician
sports merchandise sales	recreation leader	entrepreneur
stockbroker	optometrist	land developer
financial planner	pharmacist	retail sales
investor	critical care nurse	car sales

College majors

business	vocational training	English
physical education	education	journalism
health occupations		

ESTJ

ESTJs are loyal, hardworking, dependable, thorough, practical, realistic, and energetic. They value security and tradition. Because they enjoy working with people and are orderly and organized, these types like to take charge and be the leader. This personality type is often found in administrative and management positions. ESTJs work systematically and efficiently to get the job done. These types are fair, logical, and consistent. They prefer a stable and predictable environment filled with action and a variety of people.

General occupations to consider

managerial	service	professional
sales	technical	military leaders
business	agriculture	

Specific job titles

retail store manager	military officer or enlistee	physician
fire department manager	office manager	chemical engineer
small business manager	purchasing agent	auditor
restaurant manager	police officer	coach
financial or bank officer	factory supervisor	public relations worker
school principal	corrections	cook
sales manager	insurance agent	personnel or labor relations worker
top-level manager in city/ county/state government	detective	
	judge	teacher (trade, industrial, technical)
	accountant	
management consultant	nursing administrator	mortgage banker
corporate executive	mechanical engineer	

College majors

business	small business	law
business management	management	education
accounting	engineering	vocational training
finance	agriculture	

ESFP

ESFPs are practical, realistic, independent, fun, social, spontaneous, and flexible. They have great people skills and enjoy working in environments that are friendly, relaxed, and varied. They know how to have a good time and make an environment fun for others. ESFPs have a strong sense of aesthetics and are sometimes artistic and creative. They often have a special bond with people or animals. They dislike structure and routine. These types can handle many activities or projects at once.

General occupations to consider

education	health care	business and sales
social service	entertainment	service
food preparation	child care	

Specific job titles

child care worker	medical assistant	promoter
teacher (preschool,	critical care nurse	special events coordinator
elementary school,	dentist	editor or reporter
foreign languages,	dental assistant	retail merchandiser
mathematics)	exercise physiologist	fund raiser
athletic coach	dog obedience trainer	receptionist
counselor	veterinary assistant	real estate agent
library assistant	travel or tour agent	insurance agent
police officer	recreation leader or	sporting equipment sales
public health nurse	amusement site worker	retail sales
respiratory therapist	photographer	retail management
physical therapist	designer	waiter or waitress
physician	film producer	cashier
emergency medical	musician	cosmetologist
technician	performer	hairdresser
dental hygienist	actor	religious worker
chef		

College majors

education	health occupations	journalism
psychology	art	drama
foreign languages	design	music
mathematics	photography	business
physical education	English	vocational training
culinary arts	child development	

ESFJ

ESFJs are friendly, organized, hardworking, productive, conscientious, loyal, dependable, and practical. These types value harmony, stability, and security. They enjoy interacting with people and receive satisfaction from giving to others. ESFJs enjoy working in a cooperative environment in which people get along well with each other. They create order, structure, and schedules and can be depended on to complete the task at hand. They prefer to organize and control their work.

General occupations to consider

health care	social service	business
education	counseling	human resources
child care		

Specific job titles

medical or dental assistant	coach	sales representative
nurse	administrator of	hairdresser
radiologic technician	elementary	cosmetologist
dental hygienist	or secondary school	restaurant worker
speech pathologist	administrator of student	recreation or amusement
occupational therapist	personnel	site worker
dentist	child care provider	receptionist
optometrist	home economist	office manager
dietician	social worker	cashier
pharmacist	administrator of social	bank employee
physician	services	bookkeeper
physical therapist	police officer	accountant
health education	counselor	sales
practitioner	community welfare	insurance agent
medical secretary	worker	credit counselor
teacher (grades 1–12,	religious educator	merchandise planner
foreign languages,	clergy	
reading)		

College majors

health occupations	education	religious studies
biology	psychology	business
foreign languages	counseling	vocational training
English	sociology	child development

ENFP

ENFPs are friendly, creative, energetic, enthusiastic, innovative, adventurous, and fun. They have great people skills and enjoy providing service to others. They are intuitive and perceptive about people. ENFPs are good at anything that interests them and can enter a variety of fields. These types dislike routine and detailed tasks and may have difficulty following through and completing tasks. They enjoy occupations in which they can be creative and interact with people. They like a friendly and relaxed environment in which they are free to follow their inspiration and participate in adventures.

General occupations to consider

creative occupations	counseling	social service
marketing	health care	entrepreneurial business
education	religious services	arts
environmental science		

Specific job titles

journalist	public relations	physical therapist
musician	counselor	consultant
actor	clergy	inventor
entertainer	psychologist	sales
fine artist	teacher (health, special	human resources
playwright	education, English, art,	manager
newscaster	drama, music)	conference planner
reporter	social worker	employment development
interior decorator	dental hygienist	specialist
cartoonist	nurse	restaurateur
graphic designer	dietician	merchandise planner
marketing	holistic health practitioner	environmental attorney
advertising	environmentalist	lawyer

College majors

journalism	business (advertising,	religious studies
English	marketing, public	health occupations
drama	relations)	law
art	counseling	vocational training
graphic design	psychology	

ENFJ

ENFJs are friendly, sociable, empathetic, loyal, creative, imaginative, and responsible. They have great people skills and are interested in working with people and providing service to them. They are good at building harmony and cooperation and respect other people's opinions. These types can find creative solutions to problems. They are natural leaders who can make good decisions. They prefer an environment that is organized and structured and enjoy working as part of a team with other creative and caring people.

General occupations to consider

religious occupations	counseling	health care
creative occupations	education	business
communications	human services	administration

Specific job titles

director of religious	newscaster	social worker
education	politician	home economist
minister	editor	nutritionist

clergy	crisis counselor	speech pathologist
public relations	school counselor	occupational therapist
marketing	vocational or career	physical therapist
writer	counselor	optometrist
librarian	psychologist	dental hygienist
journalist	alcohol and drug	family practice physician
fine artist	counselor	psychiatrist
designer	teacher (health, art,	nursing educator
actor	drama, English, foreign	pharmacist
musician or composer	languages)	human resources trainer
fundraiser	child care worker	travel agent
recreational director	college humanities	small business executive
TV producer	professor	sales manager

College majors

religious studies	music	counseling
business (public relations,	journalism	sociology
marketing)	English	health occupations
art	foreign languages	business
graphic design	humanities	vocational training
drama	psychology	

ENTP

ENTPs are creative, ingenious, flexible, diverse, energetic, fun, motivating, logical, and outspoken. They have excellent people skills and are natural leaders, although they dislike controlling other people. They value knowledge and competence. They are lively and energetic and make good debaters and motivational speakers. They are logical and rational thinkers who can grasp complex ideas and theories. They dislike environments that are structured and rigid. These types prefer environments that allow them to engage in creative problem solving and the creation of new ideas.

General occupations to consider

creative occupations	law	health care
politics	business	architecture
engineering	science	education

Specific job titles

photographer	politician	computer professional
marketing professional	political manager	corrections officer
journalist	political analyst	sales manager
actor	social scientist	speech pathologist
writer	psychiatrist	health education
musician or composer	psychologist	practitioner
editor	engineer	respiratory therapist
reporter	construction laborer	dental assistant
advertising director	research worker	medical assistant
radio/TV talk show host	electrician	critical care nurse

producer	lawyer	counselor
art director	judge	human resources planner
new business developer	corporate executive	educator
architect		

College majors

art	music	political science
photography	business (advertising,	psychology
journalism	marketing,	health occupations
drama	management,	computers
English	human resources)	vocational training
engineering	architecture	education
science		

ENTJ

ENTJs are independent, original, visionary, logical, organized, ambitious, competitive, hardworking, and direct. They are natural leaders and organizers who identify problems and create solutions for organizations. ENTJs are often in management positions. They are good planners and accomplish goals in a timely manner. These types are logical thinkers who enjoy a structured work environment where they have opportunity for advancement. They enjoy a challenging, competitive, and exciting environment in which accomplishments are recognized.

General occupations to consider

| business | management | science |
| finance | health care | law |

Specific job titles

executive	manager in city/county/	accountant
manager	state government	auditor
supervisor	management trainer	financial manager
personnel manager	school principal	real estate agent
sales manager	bank officer	lawyer, judge
marketing manager	computer systems analyst	consultant
human resources planner	computer professional	engineer
corporate executive	credit investigator	corrections, probation
college administrator	mortgage broker	officer
health administrator	stockbroker	psychologist
small business owner	investment banker	physician
retail store manager	economist	

College majors

business management	computers	engineering
finance	law	psychology
economics	medicine	vocational training

Other Factors in Choosing a Major

Choosing your college major is one of the most difficult and important decisions you will make during your college years. After assessing their personality types, students often come up with many different options for a major and career. Future chapters will help you to think about your interests, values, and preferred lifestyle. This information will help you to narrow down your choices.

Once you have completed a thorough self-assessment, you may still have several majors to consider. At this point, it is important to do some research on the outlook for a selected career in the future and the pay you would receive. Sometimes students are disappointed after graduation when they find there are few job opportunities in their chosen career field. Sometimes students

Majors with Highest Earnings, 2014[6]*

College Major	Beginning Median Salary	Mid-Career Median Salary
Petroleum Engineering	103,000	160,000
Actuarial Mathematics	58,700	120,000
Nuclear Engineering	67,600	117,000
Chemical Engineering	68,200	115,000
Aerospace Engineering	62,800	109,000
Electrical/Computer Engineering	64,300	106,000
Computer Science	59,800	102,000
Physics	53,100	101,000
Mechanical Engineering	60,900	99,700
Materials Science & Engineering	62,700	99,500
Software Engineering	62,500	99,300
Statistics	52,500	98,900
Government	43,200	97,100
Economics	50,100	96,700
Applied Mathematics	52,800	96,200
Industrial Engineering	61,100	94,400
Management Information Systems	53,800	92,200
Biomedical Engineering	59,000	91,700
Civil Engineering	54,300	91,100
Environmental Engineering	49,400	89,800
Construction Management	51,500	88,800
Mathematics	49,400	88,800
Information Systems	51,900	87,200
Finance	49,200	87,100
Chemistry	44,100	84,100

*Includes bachelor's degrees only. Excludes medicine, law and careers requiring advanced degrees.

graduate and cannot find jobs with the salary they had hoped to earn. It is important to think about the opportunities you will have in the future. If you have several options for a career you would enjoy, you may want to consider seriously the career that has the best outlook and pay.

According to the Bureau of Labor Statistics, fields with the best outlook include health care, computers, and new "green jobs" related to preserving the environment. The top-paying careers all require math skills and include the science, engineering, computer science, health care, and business fields. Only four percent of college graduates choose the engineering and computer science fields. Since there are fewer students in these majors, the salaries are higher. If you have a talent or interest in math, you can develop this skill and use it in high-paying careers.

Other Common Majors and Earnings, 2014[7]

College Major	Beginning Median Salary	Mid-Career Median Salary
Marketing and Communications	40,200	77,600
Political Science	41,700	77,000
Architecture	41,900	75,800
Accounting	45,300	74,900
Business Administration	43,500	71,000
History	39,700	71,000
Biology	40,200	70,800
Health Sciences	38,400	70,500
Forestry	40,000	69,400
Journalism	38,100	67,700
Geography	40,800	67,200
Public Administration	40,600	66,900
English	38,700	65,200
Humanities	37,900	61,800
Psychology	36,300	60,700
Liberal Arts	36,600	60,500
Fashion Merchandising	39,100	59,100
Art History	36,900	59,000
Sociology	37,400	58,800
Criminal Justice	35,300	58,400
Fine Arts	37,400	58,200
Religious Studies	34,900	57,900
Education	37,400	55,200
Music	35,700	51,400

© 2013, SHUTTERSTOCK, INC.

Top 15 Majors That Change the World[8]*

College Major	Beginning Median Salary	Mid-Career Median Salary
Nursing	55,400	71,700
Special Education	33,800	49,600
Medical Technology	48,900	60,500
Sports Medicine	39,300	57,400
Biomedical Engineering	59,000	91,700
Athletic Training	34,800	46,900
Social Work	33,000	46,600
Child and Family Studies	30,300	37,200
Biblical Studies	35,400	50,800
Dietetics	44,200	56,600
Molecular Biology	40,400	76,400
Health Care Administration	39,300	58,600
Elementary Education	32,200	45,300
Exercise Science	32,600	51,000
Public Health	35,900	56,500

*Based on an extensive survey by Payscale at www.payscale.com by asking college graduates, "Does your work make the world a better place to live?"

Every career counselor can tell stories about students who ask, "What is the career that makes the most money? That's the career I want!" However, if you choose a career based on money alone, you might find it difficult and uninteresting for a lifetime of work. You might even find yourself retraining later in life for a job that you really enjoy. Remember that the first step is to figure out who you are and what you like. Then look at career outlook and opportunity. If you find your passion in a career that is in demand and pays well, you will probably be very happy with your career choice. If you find your passion in a career that offers few jobs and does not pay well, you will have to use your ingenuity to find a job and make a living. Many students happily make this informed choice and find a way to make it work.

"We act as though comfort and luxury were the chief requirements of life, when all that we need to make us really happy is something to be enthusiastic about."

CHARLES KINGSLEY

HAGAR © 2007 KING FEATURES SYNDICATE. WORLD RIGHTS RESERVED.

"Only passions, great
passions, can elevate the
soul to great things."
DENIS DIDEROT

Keys to Success

Find Your Passion

Mark Twain said, "The secret of success is making your vocation your vacation." Find what you like to do. Better yet, find your passion. If you can find your passion, it is easy to invest the time and effort necessary to be successful. Aviator Charles Lindbergh said, "It is the greatest shot of adrenaline to be doing what you've wanted to do so badly. You almost feel like you could fly without the plane."[9] We may not be as excited about our careers as Charles Lindbergh, but we can find careers that match our personalities and talents and provide meaning to our lives.

How do you know when you have found your passion? You have found your passion when you are doing an activity and you do not notice that the time is passing. The great painter Picasso often talked about how quickly time passed while he was painting. He said, "When I work, I relax; doing nothing or entertaining visitors makes me tired." Whether you are an artist, an athlete, a scientist, or a business entrepreneur, passion provides the energy needed to be successful. It helps you to grow and create. When you are using your talents to grow and create, you can find meaning and happiness in your life.

Psychologist Martin Seligman has written a book entitled *Authentic Happiness,* in which he writes about three types of work orientation: a job, a career, and a calling.[10] A job is what you do for the paycheck at the end of the week. Many college students have jobs to earn money for college. A career has deeper personal meaning. It involves achievement, prestige, and power. A calling is defined as "a passionate commitment to work for its own sake."[11] When you have found your calling, the job itself is the reward. He notes that people who have found their calling are consistently happier than those who have a job or even a career. One of the ways that you know you have found your calling is when you are in the state of "flow." The state of "flow" is defined as "complete absorption in an activity whose challenges mesh perfectly with your abilities."[12] People who experience "flow" are happier and more productive. They do not spend their days looking forward to Friday. Understanding your personal strengths is the beginning step to finding your calling.

Seligman adds that any job can become a calling if you use your personal strengths to do the best possible job. He cited a study of hospital cleaners. Although some viewed their job as drudgery, others viewed the job as a calling. They believed that they helped patients get better by working efficiently and anticipating the needs of doctors and nurses. They rearranged furniture and decorated walls to help patients feel better. They found their calling by applying their personal talents to their jobs. As a result, their jobs became a calling.

Sometimes we wait around for passion to find us. That probably won't happen. The first step in finding your passion is to know yourself. Then find an occupation in which you can use your talents. You may be able to find your passion by looking at your present job and finding a creative way to do it based on your special talents. It has been said that there are no dead-end jobs, just people who cannot see the possibilities. Begin your search for passion by looking at your personal strengths and how you can apply them in the job market. If the job that you have now is not your passion, see what you can learn from it and then use your skills to find a career where you are more likely to find your passion.

"Success is not the key to happiness; happiness is the key to success. If you love what you are doing, you will be successful."

ANONYMOUS

JOURNAL ENTRIES

EXPLORING YOUR PERSONALITY AND MAJOR

Go to http://www.collegesuccess1.com/JournalEntries.htm for Word files of the Journal Entries.

SUCCESS
over the Internet

Visit the *College Success Website* at http://www.collegesuccess1.com/

The *College Success Website* is continually updated with new topics and links to the material presented in this chapter. Topics include:

- Personality profiles
- Online personality assessments
- Personality types of famous people in history
- Personality types and relationships
- Personality types and marriage
- Personality and careers
- Personality and communication
- Choosing your major
- Topics just for fun

Contact your instructor if you have any problems in accessing the *College Success Website.*

Notes

1. Judith Provost and Scott Anchors, eds., *Applications of the Myers-Briggs Type Indicator in Higher Education* (Palo Alto, CA: Consulting Psychologists Press, 1991), 51.
2. Ibid., 49.
3. Otto Kroeger and Janet Thuesen, *Type Talk: The 16 Personality Types That Determine How We Live, Love and Work* (New York: Dell, 1989), 204.
4. Ibid.
5. Allen L. Hammer and Gerald P. Macdaid, *MBTI Career Report Manual* (CA: Consulting Psychologist Press, 1998), 57–89.
6. PayScale, "2013–14 College Salary Report," accessed September 2013, www.payscale.com/college-salary-report-2014/
7. Ibid.
8. Ibid.
9. Quoted in Rob Gilbert, ed., *Bits and Pieces,* December 2, 1999.
10. Martin Seligman, *Authentic Happiness* (Free Press, 2002).
11. Martin Seligman, as reported by Geoffrey Cowley, "The Science of Happiness," *Newsweek,* September 16, 2002, 49.
12. Ibid.

PERSONALITY PREFERENCES

Use the textbook and personality assessment to think about your personality type. Place an X on the scale to show your degree of preference for each dimension of personality.

Introvert _____|_____ Extravert

Sensing _____|_____ INtuitive

Thinking _____|_____ Feeling

Judging _____|_____ Perceptive

Write a key word or phrase to describe each preference.

Introvert

Extravert

Sensing

INtuitive

Thinking

Feeling

Judging

Perceptive

What careers are suggested by your personality assessment?

Was the personality assessment accurate and useful to you?

PERSONALITY SCENARIOS

Read the chapter on personality before commenting on these scenarios. Keep in mind the theory that we are all born with certain personality types and there are no good or bad types. Each type has gifts and talents that can be used to be a successful and happy person. Relate your comments to the concepts in this chapter. Your instructor may have you do this exercise as a group activity in class.

Scenario 1 (Sensing vs. Intuitive): Julie is a preschool teacher. She assigns her class to draw a picture of a bicycle. Students share their pictures with the class. One of the students has drawn a bicycle with wings. Another student laughs at the drawing and says, "Bicycles don't have wings!" How should the teacher handle this situation?

Scenario 2 (Thinking vs. Feeling): John has the almost perfect girlfriend. She is beautiful, intelligent, and fun to be with. She only has one flaw: John thinks that she is too emotional and wishes she could be a little more rational. When his girlfriend tries to talk to him about emotional issues, he analyzes her problems and proposes a logical solution. His girlfriend doesn't like the solutions that John proposes. Should John find a new girlfriend?

Scenario 3 (Introvert vs. Extravert): Mary is the mother of two children, ages five (daughter) and eight (son). The five-year-old is very social and especially enjoys birthday parties. At the last party, she invited 24 girls and they all showed up at the party. Everyone had a great time. The eight-year-old is very quiet and spends his time reading, doing artwork, building models, and hanging out with his one best friend. Mary is concerned that her son does not have very many friends. She decides to have a birthday party for her son also. The only problem is that he cannot come up with a list of children to invite to the party. What should Mary do?

Scenario 4 (Judging vs. Perceptive): Jerry and Jennifer have just been married, and they love each other very much. Jennifer likes to keep the house neat and orderly and likes to plan out activities so that there are no surprises. Jerry likes creative disorder. He leaves his things all over the house. He often comes up with creative ideas for having fun. How can Jerry and Jennifer keep their good relationship going?

Exploring Interests and Values

3

Learning
OBJECTIVES

Read to answer these key questions:

- What are my interests?

- What lifestyle do I prefer?

- How do my interests relate to possible careers?

- What are my values?

- How do I put my values into action?

Holland's Basic
Categories of Career
Interests
- Realistic
- Investigative
- Artistic
- Social
- Enterprising
- Conventional

Becoming aware of your interests and values will increase self-understanding and help you to make good decisions about your college major and future career. Interests and values are also important considerations in thinking about your preferred lifestyle.

Exploring Your Interests

Interests are simply what a person likes to do. Interests are a result of many factors, including personality, family life, values, and the environment. Knowing about your interests is helpful in planning a satisfying career. By studying people who are satisfied with their careers, psychologists have been able to help people choose careers based on their interests.

The U.S. Department of Labor has developed the O*Net Interest Profiler, which helps to identify your career interests.[1] The O*Net Interest Profiler is compatible with Holland's Theory of Vocational Personality. This is one of the most widely accepted approaches to vocational choice. According to the theory, there are six vocational personality types. These six types and their accompanying definitions are presented below.[2] As you read through each description, think about your own interests.

Realistic

People with **realistic** interests like work activities that include practical, hands-on problems and solutions. They enjoy dealing with plants, animals, and real-world materials like wood, tools, and machinery. They enjoy outside work. Often people with realistic interests do not like occupations that mainly involve doing paperwork or working closely with others.

Investigative

People with **investigative** interests like work activities that have to do with ideas and thinking more than with physical activity. They like to search for facts and figure out problems mentally rather than to persuade or lead people.

Artistic

People with **artistic** interests like work activities that deal with the artistic side of things, such as forms, designs, and patterns. They like self-expression in their work. They prefer settings where work can be done without following a clear set of rules.

Social

People with **social** interests like work activities that assist others and promote learning and personal development. They prefer to communicate more than to work with objects, machines, or data. They like to teach, give advice, help, or otherwise be of service to people.

Enterprising

People with **enterprising** interests like work activities that have to do with starting up and carrying out projects, especially business ventures. They like persuading and leading people and making decisions. They like taking risks for profit. These people prefer action rather than thought.

Conventional

People with **conventional** interests like work activities that follow set procedures and routines. They prefer working with data and detail rather than with ideas. They prefer work in which there are precise standards rather than work in which you have to judge things by yourself. These people like working where the lines of authority are clear.

According to Holland, most individuals can be described by one or more of these six personality types, frequently summarized as R-I-A-S-E-C (the first letter of each personality type). Additionally, the theory proposes that there are six corresponding work environments (or occupational groups), and that people seek out work environments that match their personality types. The better the match individuals make, the more satisfied they will be with their jobs.[3]

Holland arranged these interests on a hexagon that shows the relationship of the interests to one another. He notes that most people are not just one type, but rather a combination of types. Types that are close to each other on the hexagon are likely to have interests in common. For example, a person who is social is likely to have some artistic interests and some enterprising interests. Interests on opposite points of the hexagon are very different. For example, artistic and conventional types are opposites. Artistic types prefer freedom to be creative; conventional types prefer structure and order. The figure that follows illustrates the relationship between interest areas.[4]

> "Even if you're on the right track, you'll get run over if you just sit there."
> WILL ROGERS

> "Real success is finding your life work in work that you love."
> DAVID MCCULLOUGH

FIGURE 3.1 Relationships between interest areas.

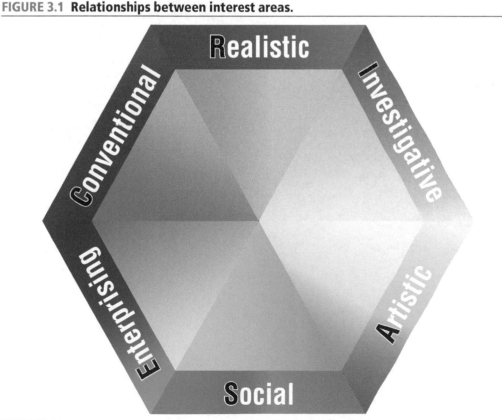

Activity

The Interest Profiler[5]

Place a checkmark next to the items in each list that you might **like to do**. Keep a positive attitude when thinking about your interests. You do not need to know how to do these activities or have the opportunity to do them to select items that you might like to do in the future. Also, be careful not to select an activity just because it is likely to produce higher income. You can earn higher income by increasing your skills and education in these areas. For example, if you would like to build a brick walkway, you could work in construction, or with more education, become a civil engineer. Just indicate what you would enjoy doing. Remember that this is not a test and that there are no right or wrong answers to the questions. The goal is for you to learn more about your personal career interests and related occupations.

When you are finished with each section, tally the number of checkmarks in each area. Sample job titles for each area of interest are included. Underline any jobs that appeal to you. You can also match your interests to over 900 occupations listed at http://www.onetonline.org/find/descriptor/browse/Interests/. This site includes information on specific occupations, including work tasks; tools and technology; knowledge, skills, and abilities required; work activities and work context; level of education required; work styles; work values; and wages and employment information.

Realistic (R)

I would like to:

_____ Build kitchen cabinets	_____ Assemble products in a factory
_____ Guard money in an armored car	_____ Catch fish as a member of a fishing crew
_____ Operate a dairy farm	_____ Refinish furniture
_____ Lay brick or tile	_____ Fix a broken faucet
_____ Monitor a machine on an assembly line	_____ Do cleaning or maintenance work
_____ Repair household appliances	_____ Maintain the grounds of a park
_____ Drive a taxi cab	_____ Operate a machine on a production line
_____ Install flooring in houses	_____ Spray trees to prevent the spread of harmful insects
_____ Raise fish in a fish hatchery	
_____ Build a brick walkway	_____ Test the quality of parts before shipment
_____ Assemble electronic parts	_____ Operate a motorboat to carry passengers
_____ Drive a truck to deliver packages to offices and homes	_____ Repair and install locks
_____ Paint houses	_____ Set up and operate machines to make products
_____ Enforce fish and game laws	_____ Put out forest fires
_____ Operate a grinding machine in a factory	
_____ Work on an offshore oil-drilling rig	
_____ Perform lawn care services	

R =

Matching Job Titles for Realistic Interests[6]
Construction worker, building contractor, cook, landscaper, housekeeper, janitor, firefighter, hazardous materials removal worker, security guard, truck driver, automotive mechanic, cardiovascular technologist, civil engineer, commercial pilot, computer support specialist, plumber, police officer, chemical engineer, fish and game warden, surveyor, archaeologist, athletic trainer, dentist, veterinarian

Investigative (I)

I would like to:

_____	Study space travel	_____	Study whales and other types of marine life
_____	Make a map of the bottom of an ocean	_____	Investigate crimes
_____	Study the history of past civilizations	_____	Study the movement of planets
_____	Study animal behavior	_____	Examine blood samples using a microscope
_____	Develop a new medicine	_____	Investigate the cause of a fire
_____	Plan a research study	_____	Study the structure of the human body
_____	Study ways to reduce water pollution	_____	Develop psychological profiles of criminals
_____	Develop a new medical treatment or procedure	_____	Develop a way to better predict the weather
_____	Determine the infection rate of a new disease	_____	Work in a biology lab
_____	Study rocks and minerals	_____	Invent a replacement for sugar
_____	Diagnose and treat sick animals	_____	Study genetics
_____	Study the personalities of world leaders	_____	Study the governments of different countries
_____	Conduct chemical experiments	_____	Do research on plants or animals
_____	Conduct biological research	_____	Do laboratory tests to identify diseases
_____	Study the population growth of a city	_____	Study weather conditions

I =

Matching Job Titles for Investigative Interests
Electronic engineering technician, emergency medical technician, fire investigator, paralegal, police detective, engineer (aerospace, biomedical, chemical, electrical, computer, environmental, or industrial), chemist, computer systems analyst, geoscientist, market research analyst, anesthesiologist, biochemist, biophysicist, clinical psychologist, dietician, physician, microbiologist, pharmacist, psychiatrist, surgeon, veterinarian, science teacher, college professor

Artistic (A)

I would like to:

_____	Conduct a symphony orchestra	_____	Create dance routines for a show
_____	Write stories or articles for magazines	_____	Write books or plays
_____	Direct a play	_____	Play a musical instrument

_____ Perform comedy routines in front of an audience

_____ Perform as an extra in movies, plays, or television shows

_____ Write reviews of books or plays

_____ Compose or arrange music

_____ Act in a movie

_____ Dance in a Broadway show

_____ Draw pictures

_____ Sing professionally

_____ Perform stunts for a movie or television show

_____ Create special effects for movies

_____ Conduct a musical choir

_____ Act in a play

_____ Paint sets for plays

_____ Audition singers and musicians for a musical show

_____ Design sets for plays

_____ Announce a radio show

_____ Write scripts for movies or television shows

_____ Write a song

_____ Perform jazz or tap dance

_____ Direct a movie

_____ Sing in a band

_____ Design artwork for magazines

_____ Edit movies

_____ Pose for a photographer

A =

Matching Job Titles for Artistic Interests

Model, actor, fine artist, floral designer, singer, tile setter, architectural drafter, architect, dancer, fashion designer, film and video editor, hairdresser, makeup artist, museum technician, music composer, photographer, self-enrichment education teacher, art director, broadcast news analyst, choreographer, editor, graphic designer, landscape architect, creative writer, public relations specialist, teacher (of art, drama, or music)

Social (S)

I would like to:

_____ Teach an individual an exercise routine

_____ Perform nursing duties in a hospital

_____ Give CPR to someone who has stopped breathing

_____ Help people with personal or emotional problems

_____ Teach children how to read

_____ Work with mentally disabled children

_____ Teach an elementary school class

_____ Give career guidance to people

_____ Supervise the activities of children at a camp

_____ Help people with family-related problems

_____ Perform rehabilitation therapy

_____ Do volunteer work at a nonprofit organization

_____ Help elderly people with their daily activities

_____ Teach children how to play sports

_____ Help disabled people improve their daily living skills

_____ Teach sign language to people with hearing disabilities

_____ Help people who have problems with drugs or alcohol

_____ Help conduct a group therapy session

_____ Help families care for ill relatives

_____ Provide massage therapy to people

_____ Plan exercises for disabled patients

_____ Counsel people who have a life-threatening illness

_____ Teach disabled people work and living skills

_____ Organize activities at a recreational facility

_____ Take care of children at a day care center

_____ Organize field trips for disabled people

_____ Assist doctors in treating patients

_____ Work with juveniles on probation

_____ Provide physical therapy to people recovering from injuries

_____ Teach a high school class

S =

Matching Job Titles for Social Interests

Host, hostess, bartender, lifeguard, food server, child care worker, home health aide, occupational therapist, occupational therapist aide, personal and home care aide, physical therapist, physical therapist aide, veterinary assistant, dental hygienist, fitness trainer, medical assistant, nanny, teacher (preschool, kindergarten, elementary, middle, or high school), registered nurse, respiratory therapist, self-enrichment education teacher, tour guide, mediator, educational administrator, health educator, park naturalist, probation officer, recreation worker, chiropractor, clergy, counseling psychologist, social worker, substance abuse counselor, physician assistant, speech and language pathologist

Enterprising (E)

I would like to:

_____ Buy and sell stocks and bonds

_____ Manage a retail store

_____ Sell telephone and other communication equipment

_____ Operate a beauty salon or barber shop

_____ Sell merchandise over the telephone

_____ Run a stand that sells newspapers and magazines

_____ Give a presentation about a product you are selling

_____ Buy and sell land

_____ Sell compact discs at a music store

_____ Run a toy store

_____ Manage the operations of a hotel

_____ Sell houses

_____ Sell candy and popcorn at sports events

_____ Manage a supermarket

_____ Manage a department within a large company

_____ Sell a soft drink product line to stores and restaurants

_____ Sell refreshments at a movie theater

_____ Sell hair-care products to stores and salons

_____ Start your own business

_____ Negotiate business contracts

_____ Represent a client in a lawsuit

_____ Negotiate contracts for professional athletes

_____ Be responsible for the operation of a company

_____ Market a new line of clothing

_____ Sell newspaper advertisements

_____ Sell merchandise at a department store

_____ Sell automobiles

_____ Manage a clothing store

_____ Sell restaurant franchises to individuals

_____ Sell computer equipment to a store

E =

Matching Job Titles

Cashier, food worker, customer service representative, sales worker, supervisor, gaming dealer, inspector, retail sales clerk, chef, food service manager, operations manager, real estate broker, realtor, sheriff, wholesale or retail buyer, advertiser, appraiser, construction manager, criminal investigator, financial manager, insurance sales agent, meeting and convention planner, personal financial advisor, sales engineer, judge, lawyer, business or political science teacher, educational administrator, librarian, medical health manager, treasurer, controller

Conventional (C)

I would like to:

_____ Develop a spreadsheet using computer software

_____ Proofread records or forms

_____ Use a computer program to generate customer bills

_____ Schedule conferences for an organization

_____ Keep accounts payable/receivable for an office

_____ Load computer software into a large computer network

_____ Transfer funds between banks using a computer

_____ Organize and schedule office meetings

_____ Use a word processor to edit and format documents

_____ Operate a calculator

_____ Direct or transfer phone calls for a large organization

_____ Perform office filing tasks

_____ Compute and record statistical and other numerical data

_____ Generate the monthly payroll checks for an office

_____ Take notes during a meeting

_____ Keep shipping and receiving records

_____ Calculate the wages of employees

_____ Assist senior-level accountants in performing bookkeeping tasks

_____ Type labels for envelopes and packages

_____ Inventory supplies using a handheld computer

_____ Develop an office filing system

_____ Keep records of financial transactions for an organization

_____ Record information from customers applying for charge accounts

_____ Photocopy letters and reports

_____ Record rent payments

_____ Enter information into a database

_____ Keep inventory records

_____ Maintain employee records

_____ Stamp, sort, and distribute mail for an organization

_____ Handle customers' bank transactions

C =

Matching Job Titles for Conventional Interests

Cashier, cook, janitor, landscaping worker, resort desk clerk, medical records technician, medical secretary, bookkeeping and accounting clerk, dental assistant, drafter, loan officer, paralegal, pharmacy technician, purchasing agent, accountant, auditor, budget analyst, city and regional planner, computer security specialist, cost estimator, credit analyst, database administrator, environmental compliance inspector, financial analyst, geophysical data technician, librarian, proofreader, computer science teacher, pharmacist, statistician, treasurer

Summing Up Your Results

Put the number of checkmarks from each section of the Interest Profiler on the lines that follow:

____ Realistic   ____ Social

____ Investigative   ____ Enterprising

____ Artistic   ____ Conventional

What are your top three areas of interest? (Realistic, Investigative, Artistic, Social, Enterprising, Conventional?)

1. _____

2. _____

3. _____

Journal Entry

List your top three areas of interest from the Interest Profiler (realistic, investigative, social, enterprising, or conventional). Go to http://www.onetonline.org/find/descriptor/browse/interests/ and click on your highest interests to find some matching careers. List one career and briefly describe the education required, salary, and projected growth for one of these careers. Here is an easy outline:

My top interests on the Interest Profiler are . . . .

One career that matches my interests is . . .

The education required is . . .

The median annual salary is . . .

FIGURE 3.2 Lifestyle Triangle.[7]

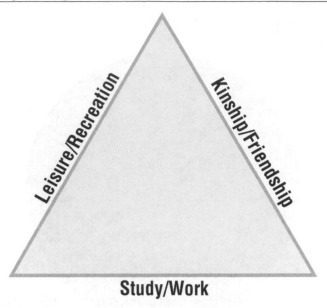

Interests and Lifestyle

Our occupational interests determine what we study and the kinds of occupations we choose. While study and work form the basis of our lifestyle, there are other important components. What we choose to do for fun and relaxation helps us to be refreshed and keeps life interesting. Another component of a balanced lifestyle is time spent with friends and family. It is important to choose work that allows you to have the resources and time to lead a balanced lifestyle with all of these components. A balanced lifestyle has been described as a triangle with work and study forming the base, leisure and recreation forming one side, and kinship and friendship forming the other side.

Give some thought to the kind of lifestyle you prefer. Think about balancing your work, leisure, and social activities.

Journal Entry

In seeking to accomplish lifetime goals, sometimes people are not successful because they place too much emphasis on work, study, leisure, or social life. How would you balance work, study, leisure, and social life to achieve your lifetime goals?

2

Quiz

Interests

Test what you have learned by selecting the correct answers to the following questions.

1. Realistic people are likely to choose a career in
    a. construction or engineering.
    b. accounting or real estate.
    c. financial investments or banking.

2. Investigative people are likely to choose a career in
    a. art or music.
    b. teaching or social work.
    c. science or laboratory work.

3. Enterprising people are likely to choose a career in
    a. computer programming or accounting.
    b. business management or government.
    c. health care or social services.

4. Conventional people are likely to choose a career in
    a. health care or social services.
    b. financial investments or banking.
    c. manufacturing or transportation.

5. Social types generally
    a. enjoy working with tools and machines.
    b. are humanistic and idealistic.
    c. have skills in selling and communication.

How did you do on the quiz? Check your answers: 1. a, 2. c, 3. b, 4. b, 5. b

Using Values to Make Important Life Decisions

Values are what we think is important and what we feel is right and good. Values come from many sources, including our parents, friends, the media, our religious background, our culture, our society, and the historical time in which we live. Our values make us different and unique individuals. Knowing our values helps us to make good decisions about work and life. For example, consider a situation in which a person is offered a high-paying job that involves a high degree of responsibility and a lot of stress. If the person values challenge and excitement and views stress as a motivator, the chances are that it would be a good decision to take the job. If the person values peace of mind and has a difficult time coping with stress, it might be better to forgo the higher income and maintain quality of life. Making decisions consistent with our values is one of the keys to happiness and success.

Values and needs are closely related. Humanistic psychologist Abraham Maslow[8] theorized that we adopt certain values to fulfill psychological or physical needs. He described needs and values in terms of a pyramid in which needs are organized in a hierarchy arranged from the most basic to the most complex and personal. We cannot move to the next higher level until lower-level needs are met. These needs, listed in order from most basic to most complex, can be defined as follows:

*   **Biological needs.** Basic needs for survival, including food, water, air, and clothing.
*   **Safety needs.** Basic needs for shelter and a safe and predictable environment.
*   **Love and belongingness.** Includes love, respect, and caring from our family and friends.
*   **Self-esteem.** Feeling good about yourself and having confidence in your abilities.
*   **Intellectual.** Having the knowledge and understanding needed for survival.
*   **Aesthetic.** Having an appreciation of beauty.
*   **Self-actualization.** Developing and reaching your fullest potential, enabling you to contribute to society.

FIGURE 3.3 Maslow's Hierarchy of Needs.

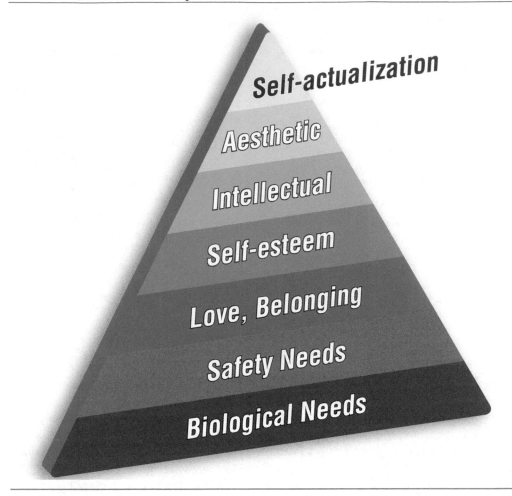

An example of a practical application of this theory is finding a solution for home-less people in society. It is easy to say that they should just go get jobs. Applying Maslow's hierarchy of needs, we would say that the first step in helping the homeless is to meet their biological needs. Before they can worry about employment, they need food, water, and clothing. Next, they need shelter so they have a safe and predictable environment. They need to know that people care about them so they can develop self-esteem. Once people have self-esteem and confidence, they can begin to be trained and educated. Once they have skills, they can become employed and enjoy the good life, appreciate beauty, and reach their potential. A person who is employed pays taxes and may do volunteer work to contribute to society.

Self-actualization is another word for success. It means knowing about and using your talents to fulfill your potential. It means being healthy and creative. It is being the best that you can be. Abraham Maslow said, "We may still often (if not always) ex-pect that a new discontent and restlessness will soon develop, unless the individual is doing what he's fitted for. A musician must make music, an artist must paint, a poet must write, if he's to be ultimately at peace. What a person can be, he must be. This need we call self-actualization."[9]

We are all ultimately aiming for self-actualization. Here are some characteristics of the self-actualized person:

- Feels secure, loved, and respected, and makes a connection with others,
- Values self and others,
- Is independent,
- Can make decisions and accept responsibility,
- Appreciates other people and cares for the world,
- Is open to new ideas,
- Resists conformity,
- Has little need for status symbols,
- Is emotionally balanced,
- Is not burdened with anxiety, guilt, or shame,
- Treats others with respect,
- Feels at one with humankind,
- Has deep and caring relationships,
- Can look at life with a sense of humor,
- Is creative, passionate, and enjoys life,
- Takes time for self-renewal and relaxation,
- Has strong values and a philosophy of life.

This sounds great, but may be difficult to achieve. Remember that we are always on the road to self-actualization. Life is about growing and changing. If we do not grow and change, life becomes boring. It all begins with basic needs for survival. Once we have the basic needs for survival, we can focus on wants or desires (the possibilities). We can't have everything, so we determine what is important or what we value the most. Knowing what we value helps us to make good decisions about life goals. In setting our goals, we put values into practice. Meeting the challenges of our lives and accomplishing our goals lead to satisfaction and happiness. The process looks like this:

FIGURE 3.4 Meeting the challenges of our lives and accomplishing our goals lead to satisfaction and happiness.

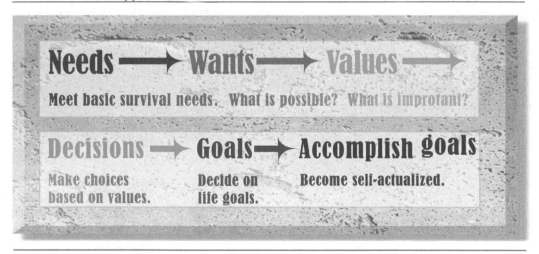

Needs ⟶ Wants ⟶ Values ⟶
Meet basic survival needs. What is possible? What is important?

Decisions ⟶ Goals ⟶ Accomplish goals
Make choices based on values. Decide on life goals. Become self-actualized.

"Try not to be a man of success, but rather to become a man of value."
ALBERT EINSTEIN

Journal
Entry

Review Maslow's theory of self-actualization. How would you apply Maslow's theory to being successful in life?

3

Activity

Values Checklists

Assessing Your Personal Values

Use the following checklist to begin to think about what values are important to you.
Place a checkmark next to any value that is important to you. There are no right or wrong answers. If you think of other values that are important to you, add them to the bottom of the list.

——— Having financial security

——— Making a contribution to humankind

——— Being a good parent

——— Being honest

——— Acquiring wealth

——— Being a wise person

——— Becoming an educated person

——— Believing in a higher power (God)

——— Preserving civil rights

——— Never being bored

——— Enjoying life and having fun

——— Making something out of my life

——— Being an ethical person

——— Feeling safe and secure

——— Having a good marriage

——— Having good friends

——— Having social status

——— Being patriotic

——— Having power

——— Having good morals

——— Being creative

——— Having control over my life

——— Growing and developing

——— Feeling competent

——— Feeling relaxed

——— Having prestige

——— Having good family relationships

——— Preserving the environment

——— Having the respect of others

——— Becoming famous

——— Happiness

——— Freedom and independence

——— Common sense

——— Having pride in my culture

——— Doing community service

——— Achieving my goals in life

——— Having adventures

——— Having leisure time

——— Having good health

——— Being loyal

——— Having a sense of accomplishment

——— Participating in church activities

——— Being physically fit

——— Helping others

——— Being a good person

——— Having time to myself

——— Loving and being loved

——— Being physically attractive

——— Achieving something important

——— Accepting who I am

——— Appreciating natural beauty

——— Using my artistic talents

——— Improving society

——— Having good mental health

——— Being a good athlete

——— Enjoying the present moment

——— Maintaining peace of mind

——— Feeling good about myself

——— Making a difference

——— Other: _____

——— Other: _____

——— Other: _____

Journal Entry

What is your most important value? Why is it important to you?

Quiz

Values

1. To make a good decision, it is important to be aware of your values. Values describe

    a. how you spend your money.
    b. what you think is important.
    c. the best buy for your money.

2. According to Maslow, people who have reached their highest potential are

    a. self-motivated.
    b. famous.
    c. self-actualized.

3. According to Maslow, homeless people would have difficulty finding a job unless they

    a. had their biological and safety needs met.
    b. had a better work ethic.
    c. became self-actualized.

4. It is important to choose work that allows you to lead a balanced lifestyle that includes time for

    a. leisure, socializing, and study/work.
    b. fun, socializing, and following your own interests.
    c. work, study, and time for yourself.

5. To act on your values means to

    a. get good value for your money.
    b. treat others with respect.
    c. act in a manner consistent with your values.

How did you do on the quiz? Check your answers: 1. b, 2. c, 3. a, 4. a, 5. c

Keys to Success
Act on Your Values

Values are what are most important to you; they are your highest principles. They provide the road map to your success and happiness. You will face important turning points along life's journey. Should I go to college? What will be my major? What career will I have? Whom should I marry? What job should I take? Where shall I live? You can find good answers to these questions by being aware of your values and using them to make decisions and guide your actions. If your decisions follow your values, you can get what you want out of life.

The first step is knowing your values. You may need some time to think about your values and change them if they are not right for you. What values were you taught as a child? What values do you want to keep as an adult? Look around at people that you admire. What are their values? What values have you learned from your religion? Are these values important to you? Ask your friends about their values and share yours. Revise and rethink your values periodically. Make sure your values are your own and not necessarily values that someone has told you were important. When you begin to think about values, you can come up with many things that are important. The key is to find out which values are most important. In this way, when you are faced with a choice, you will not be confused. You will know what is most important to you.

Knowing about values is not enough. It is important to act consistently with your values and to follow them. For example, if people value health but continue to smoke, they are saying one thing but doing another. If they value family but spend all of their time at work, they are not acting consistently with their values. As a result, they might find that their family is gone and they have lost something that is really valuable.

"The great aim of education is not knowledge, but action."

HERBERT SPENCER

Use your actions to question or reaffirm your values. Do you really value your health and family? If so, take action to preserve your good health and spend time with your family. It is necessary to periodically look at your patterns of behavior. Do you act out of habit or do you act according to what is important to you? Habits might need to be changed to get what you value most out of life.

In times of doubt and difficulty, your values can keep you going. If you truly value getting a college education, you can put in the effort to accomplish your goal. When you have doubts about whether you can be successful, examine your values again and remind yourself of why you are doing what you are doing. For example, if you value being an independent business entrepreneur, you will put in the effort to be successful. If you value being a good parent, you will find the patience and develop the skill to succeed. Reminding yourself of your values can help you to continue your commitment to accomplishing your goals.

By knowing your values and following them, you have a powerful tool for making decisions, taking action, and motivating yourself to be successful.

JOURNAL ENTRIES
EXPLORING INTERESTS AND VALUES

Go to http://www.collegesuccess1.com/JournalEntries.htm for Word files of the Journal Entries.

SUCCESS
over the Internet

Visit the *College Success Website* at http://www.collegesuccess1.com/

The *College Success Website* is continually updated with new topics and links to the material presented in this chapter. Topics include:

- Occupations for realistic, investigative, artistic, social, enterprising, and conventional interests
- Holland's self-directed search
- Various self-assessments
- Being a self-actualized person

Contact your instructor if you have any problems in accessing the *College Success Website*.

Notes

1. U.S. Department of Labor, "O*Net Interest Profiler," available at http://onetcenter.org
2. U.S. Department of Labor, "O*Net Interest Profiler User's Guide," available at http://onetcenter.org
3. John L. Holland, *Making Vocational Choices: A Theory of Vocational Personalities and Work Environments* (2nd Ed.), (Englewood Cliffs, NJ: Prentice-Hall, 1985).
4. U.S. Department of Labor, "O*Net Interest Profiler User's Guide."
5. Adapted from U.S. Department of Labor, "O*Net Interest Profiler."
6. Job titles in this section from http://www.onetonline.org/find/descriptor/browse/interests/
7. The Lifestyle Triangle adapted with permission from NTL Institute, "Urban Middle-Class Lifestyles in Transition," by Paula Jean Miller and Gideon Sjoberg, *Journal of Applied Behavioral Science* 9 (1973), nos. 2/3: 149.
8. Abraham Maslow, *Motivation and Personality* (New York: Harper and Row, 1970).
9. Maslow, *Motivation and Personality*, 91.

VALUES IN ACTION

Knowing your values is important in order to make good decisions. Read the following scenarios and think about the values of the person described. Make a recommendation to answer the question posed in each case. You may want to do this exercise in a group with other students.

Scenario 1: What major should I choose? Shawn is 20 years old and has completed two years of college. He has been trying to decide whether to major in engineering or music. He has completed all of his general education requirements as well as several courses in music, math, and physics. As a child, Shawn was interested in science and dreamed of making new inventions. He always took things apart to see how they worked. Math was always easy for Shawn, and he received awards for achievement in science.

He also took part in band throughout his school years and learned to play several instruments. As a teenager, he had a garage band and became so interested in playing the piano that he spent two hours a day practicing. Shawn's dilemma was that he was becoming stressed out trying to do both majors and no longer had time to do well in both music and engineering. He also wanted to have time to get a part-time job in order to become more independent. Shawn's top five values are being independent and living on his own, having a secure future, doing interesting work, achieving something important, and being able to relax.

What are Shawn's values?

What major should Shawn consider? Why?

Scenario 2: Should I continue my education? Maria is a married mother of two young boys, ages five and seven, and a part-time college student. Maria and her husband, Juan, are very proud of their Mexican heritage and value their marriage and family. They both think that it is important for Maria to spend time with the children. Maria learned to speak English as a second language and has made sure that her children speak both English and Spanish. While the children are in school, Maria has been attending college part-time with the goal of becoming a teacher's aide in a class for bilingual children. She has some experience as a teacher's aide and gets a great deal of satisfaction from helping the children.

Juan works in construction, and the family has sacrificed to come up with the money to pay for Maria to attend college. Maria has struggled to earn her associate's degree and is proud of her accomplishments. She values her education and wants her children to do well in school. Now Maria is considering continuing her education to earn the bachelor's degree so that she can become a teacher. She would enjoy having her own classroom, loves working with children, and would have a higher income as a teacher than she would as a teacher's aide. Maria's husband is concerned that she will spend too much time at college and will not be home for the children. He is also relieved that Maria has finished college and plans to work part-time to supplement the family income while the children are in school.

What are Maria's values? Should Maria continue her education?

TWENTY THINGS YOU LIKE TO DO

Your instructor may ask you to do this exercise in class. In five minutes, see if you can make a list of 20 things that you like to do. To help you with this list, think about the following questions:

- What do you like to do for fun in the summer? fall? winter? spring?
- What do you like to do with your family? friends?
- What do you like to do on vacation?
- What do you like to do on a rainy day when you are home alone?
- What do you like to do to relax?
- What kinds of physical activities do you like?
- What are your hobbies?
- What do you like to do at school? at work?

_____ 1. _____

_____ 2. _____

_____ 3. _____

_____ 4. _____

_____ 5. _____

_____ 6. _____

_____ 7. _____

_____ 8. _____

_____ 9. _____

_____ 10. _____

_____ 11. _____

_____ 12. _____

_____ 13. _____

_____ 14. _____

_____ 15. _____

_____ 16. _____

_____ 17. _____

_____ 18. _____

_____ 19. _____

_____ 20. _____

Write one or more of these symbols to the left of each item.

$ For activities that cost more than $20 each time you do them

P   For things that you do with people

I   For things that you do by yourself

T   For activities that involve working with things (e.g., gardening, crafts, working on your car)

D   For activities that involve working with data (e.g., working with your computer, doing budgeting, filing, organizing)

A   For activities that involve some physical activity

R   For activities that involve risk or adventure (e.g., car racing, skydiving, skiing)

MT   For activities that you would like to have more time to do

1–5   For the five most important activities, with 1 being most important

After labeling the items in your list, answer the following lifestyle questions.

1. Look at the number of items with a $ sign. How important is money to your lifestyle? Do you need a high-paying occupation, or could you take a job that pays less but offers great personal satisfaction?

2. Do you like to do things with people, things, or data? Can you see a pattern? Would you prefer to work with people or alone? Do you have the same preference for your leisure time?

3. Are you physically active? Do you enjoy risk and adventure?

4. Which items do you wish you had more time to do?

5. Look at the top five items that you selected. Why are they important to your lifestyle?

LIFESTYLE TRIANGLE

Look at the items you selected in the exercise "Twenty Things You Like to Do." Separate them into the following categories and list them below.

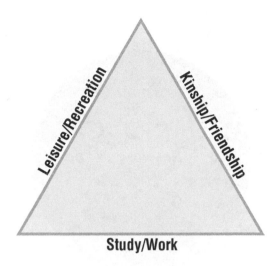

Leisure/Recreation	Study/Work	Kinship/Friendship

How balanced is your lifestyle? Do you need to add more activities in any of the categories?

In the future, my lifestyle will be . . .

SUMMING UP VALUES

Look at the "Values Checklist" you completed in this chapter. Choose the 10 values most important to you and list them here.

_____   _____

_____   _____

_____   _____

_____   _____

_____   _____

Next, pick out the value that is most important and label it 1. Label your second most important value 2, and so on, until you have picked out your top five values.

1. My most important value is _____ .
   Why?

2. My second most important value is _____ .
   Why?

3. My third most important value is _____ .
   Why?

4. My fourth most important value is _____ .
   Why?

5. My fifth most important value is _____ .
   Why?

Exploring Your Multiple Intelligences

4

Learning
OBJECTIVES

Read to answer these key questions:

- What are multiple intelligences?

- What kinds of intelligence do I have?

- What are my personal strengths?

- What is emotional intelligence?

- What are my goals for the future?

- How can I create the future I want for myself?

What Are Multiple Intelligences?

In 1904, the French psychologist Alfred Binet developed the IQ test, which provided a single score to measure intelligence. This once widely used and accepted test came into question because it measured the intelligence of individuals in schools in a particular culture. In different cultures and different situations, the test was less valid. As an alternative to traditional IQ tests, Harvard professor Howard Gardner developed the theory of multiple intelligences.[1] He looked at intelligence in a broader and more inclusive way than people had done in the past.

Howard Gardner observed famous musicians, artists, athletes, scientists, inventors, naturalists, and others who were recognized contributors to society to formulate a more meaningful definition of intelligence. He defined intelligence as **the human ability to solve problems or design or compose something valued in at least one culture**. His definition broadens the scope of human potential. He identified nine different intelligences: musical, interpersonal, logical-mathematical, spatial, bodily-kinesthetic, linguistic, intrapersonal, naturalist, and existential. He selected these intelligences because they are all represented by an area in the brain and are valued in different cultures. His theory can help us to understand and appreciate many different kinds of talents.

These intelligences are measured by looking at performance in activities associated with each intelligence. A key idea in this theory is that most people can develop all of their intelligences and become relatively competent in each area. Another key idea is that these intelligences work together in complex ways to make us unique. For example, an athlete uses bodily-kinesthetic intelligence to run, kick, or jump. They use spatial intelligence to keep their eye on the ball and hit it. They also need linguistic and interpersonal skills to be good members of a team.

Developing intelligences is a product of three factors:

1. Biological endowment based on heredity and genetics

2. Personal life history

3. Cultural and historical background[2]

For example, Wolfgang Amadeus Mozart was born with musical talent (biological endowment). Members of his family were musicians who encouraged Mozart in music (personal life history). Mozart lived in Europe during a time when music flourished and wealthy patrons were willing to pay composers (cultural and historical background).

Each individual's life history contains **crystallizers** that promote the development of the intelligences and **paralyzers** that inhibit the development of the intelligences. These crystallizers and paralyzers often take place in early childhood. For example, Einstein was given a magnetic compass when he was four years old. He became so interested in the compass that he started on his journey of exploring the universe. An example of a paralyzer is being embarrassed or feeling humiliated about your math skills in elementary school so that you begin to lose confidence in your ability to do math. Paralyzers involve shame, guilt, fear, and anger and prevent intelligence from being developed.

This textbook includes an access code for taking the MI Advantage, which assesses multiple intelligences, provides a profile of your individual strengths, and matches your results to careers with links to online career information. As you take this assessment, think positively about your skills. The following information and activities help to gain a deeper understanding of your multiple intelligences and related skills along with matching careers.

"I have no special talent. I am only passionately curious."

ALBERT EINSTEIN

Journal
Entry

Look at your results from the MI Advantage multiple intelligences assessment. According to this assessment, what are your highest multiple intelligences? List any suggested careers in which you are interested.

1

Activity

Describing Your Multiple Intelligences

Below are some definitions and examples of the different intelligences. As you read each section, think positively about your intelligence in this area. Place a checkmark in front of each item that is true for you.

Musical

Musical intelligence involves hearing and remembering musical patterns and manipulating patterns in music. Some occupations connected with this intelligence include musician, performer, composer, and music critic. Place a checkmark next to each skill that you possess in this area.

_____ I enjoy singing, humming, or whistling.

_____ One of my interests is playing recorded music.

_____ I have collections of recorded music.

_____ I play or used to play a musical instrument.

_____ I can play the drums or tap out rhythms.

_____ I appreciate music.

_____ Music affects how I feel.

_____ I enjoy having music on while working or studying.

_____ I can clap my hands and keep time to music.

_____ I can tell when a musical note is off key.

_____ I remember melodies and the words to songs.

_____ I have participated in a band, chorus, or other musical group.

Look at the items you have checked above and summarize your musical intelligence.

_____

_____

_____

Interpersonal

Interpersonal intelligence is defined as understanding people. Occupations connected with this intelligence involve working with people and helping them, as in education or health care. Place a checkmark next to each skill that you possess in this area.

_____ I enjoy being around people.

_____ I am sensitive to other people's feelings.

_____ I am a good listener.

_____ I understand how others feel.

_____ I have many friends.

_____ I enjoy parties and social gatherings.

_____ I enjoy participating in groups.

_____ I can get people to cooperate and work together.

_____ I am involved in clubs or community activities.

_____ People come to me for advice.

_____ I am a peacemaker.

_____ I enjoy helping others.

Look at the items you have checked above and summarize your interpersonal intelligence.

_____

_____

_____

Logical-Mathematical

Logical-mathematical intelligence involves understanding abstract principles and manipulating numbers, quantities, and operations. Some examples of occupations associated with logical-mathematical intelligence are mathematician, tax accountant, scientist, and computer programmer. Place a checkmark next to each skill that you possess. Keep an open mind. People usually either love or hate this area.

_____ I can do arithmetic problems quickly.

_____ I enjoy math.

_____ I enjoy doing puzzles.

_____ I enjoy working with computers.

_____ I am interested in computer programming.

_____ I enjoy science classes.

_____ I enjoy doing the experiments in lab science courses.

_____ I can look at information and outline it easily.

_____ I understand charts and diagrams.

_____ I enjoy playing chess or checkers.

_____ I use logic to solve problems.

_____ I can organize things and keep them in order.

Look at the items you have checked above and summarize your logical-mathematical intelligence.

_____

_____

_____

Spatial

Spatial intelligence involves the ability to manipulate objects in space. For example, a baseball player uses spatial intelligence to hit a ball. Occupations associated with spatial intelligence include pilot, painter, sculptor, architect, inventor, and surgeon. This intelligence is often used in athletics, the arts, or the sciences. Place a checkmark next to each skill that you possess in this area.

_____ I can appreciate a good photograph or piece of art.

_____ I think in pictures and images.

_____ I can use visualization to remember.

_____ I can easily read maps, charts, and diagrams.

_____ I participate in artistic activities (art, drawing, painting, photography).

_____ I know which way is north, south, east, and west.

_____ I can put things together.

_____ I enjoy jigsaw puzzles or mazes.

_____ I enjoy seeing movies, slides, or photographs.

_____ I can appreciate good design.

_____ I enjoy using telescopes, microscopes, or binoculars.

_____ I understand color, line, shape, and form.

Look at the items you have checked above and summarize your spatial intelligence.

_____

_____

_____

Bodily-Kinesthetic

Bodily-kinesthetic intelligence is defined as being able to use your body to solve problems. People with bodily-kinesthetic intelligence make or invent objects or perform. They learn by doing, touching, and handling. Occupations connected to this type of intelligence include athlete, performer (dancer, actor), craftsperson, sculptor, mechanic, and surgeon. Place a checkmark next to each skill that you possess in this area.

_____ I am good at using my hands.

_____ I have good coordination and balance.

_____ I learn best by moving around and touching things.

_____ I participate in physical activities or sports.

_____ I learn new sports easily.

_____ I enjoy watching sports events.

_____ I am skilled in a craft such as woodworking, sewing, art, or fixing machines.

_____ I have good manual dexterity.

_____ I find it difficult to sit still for a long time.

_____ I prefer to be up and moving.

_____ I am good at dancing and remember dance steps easily.

_____ It was easy for me to learn to ride a bike or skateboard.

Look at the items you checked above and describe your bodily-kinesthetic intelligence.

_____

_____

_____

Linguistic

People with linguistic intelligence are good with language and words. They have good reading, writing, and speaking skills. Linguistic intelligence is an asset in any occupation. Specific related careers include writing, education, and politics. Place a checkmark next to each skill that you possess in this area.

_____ I am a good writer.

_____ I am a good reader.

_____ I enjoy word games and crossword puzzles.

_____ I can tell jokes and stories.

_____ I am good at explaining.

_____ I can remember names, places, facts, and trivia.

_____ I'm generally good at spelling.

_____ I have a good vocabulary.

_____ I read for fun and relaxation.

_____ I am good at memorizing.

_____ I enjoy group discussions.

_____ I have a journal or diary.

Look at the items you have checked above and summarize your linguistic intelligence.

_____

_____

_____

Intrapersonal

Intrapersonal intelligence is the ability to understand yourself and how to best use your natural talents and abilities. Examples of careers associated with this intelligence include novelist, psychologist, or being self-employed. Place a checkmark next to each skill that you possess in this area.

_____ I understand and accept my strengths and weaknesses.

_____ I am very independent.

_____ I am self-motivated.

_____ I have definite opinions on controversial issues.

_____ I enjoy quiet time alone to pursue a hobby or work on a project.

_____ I am self-confident.

_____ I can work independently.

_____ I can help others with self-understanding.

_____ I appreciate quiet time for concentration.

_____ I am aware of my own feelings and sensitive to others.

_____ I am self-directed.

_____ I enjoy reflecting on ideas and concepts.

Look at the items you have checked above and summarize your intrapersonal intelligence.

_____

_____

_____

Naturalist

The naturalist is able to recognize, classify, and analyze plants, animals, and cultural artifacts. Occupations associated with this intelligence include botanist, horticulturist, biologist, archeologist, and environmental occupations. Place a checkmark next to each skill you possess in this area.

_____ I know the names of minerals, plants, trees, and animals.

_____ I think it is important to preserve our natural environment.

_____ I enjoy taking classes in the natural sciences such as biology.

_____ I enjoy the outdoors.

_____ I take care of flowers, plants, trees, or animals.

_____ I am interested in archeology or geology.

_____ I would enjoy a career involved in protecting the environment.

_____ I have or used to have a collection of rocks, shells, or insects.

_____ I belong to organizations interested in protecting the environment.

_____ I think it is important to protect endangered species.

_____ I enjoy camping or hiking.

_____ I appreciate natural beauty.

Look at the items you have checked above and describe your naturalist intelligence.

_____

_____

_____

Existential

Existential intelligence is the capacity to ask profound questions about the meaning of life and death. This intelligence is the cornerstone of art, religion, and philosophy. Related occupations include minister, philosopher, psychologist, and artist. Place a checkmark next to each skill that you possess in this area.

_____ I often think about the meaning and purpose of life.

_____ I have strong personal beliefs and convictions.

_____ I enjoy thinking about abstract theories.

_____ I have considered being a philosopher, scientist, theologian, or artist.

_____ I often read books that are philosophical or imaginative.

_____ I enjoy reading science fiction.

_____ I like to work independently.

_____ I like to search for meaning in my studies.

_____ I wonder if there are other intelligent life forms in the universe.

Look at the items you have checked above and describe your existential intelligence.

_____

_____

_____

Journal Entry

Look at the above charts and see where you have the most checkmarks. What do you think are your highest intelligences? Do your opinions match the results on the MI Advantage multiple intelligences assessment?

2

Build on Your Strengths

Consider your personal strengths when deciding on a career. People in each of the multiple intelligence areas have different strengths:

- Musical strengths include listening to music, singing, playing a musical instrument, keeping a beat, and recognizing musical patterns. People with this intelligence are "musical smart."

- Interpersonal strengths include communication skills, social skills, helping others, understanding others' feelings, and the ability to resolve conflicts. People with this intelligence are "people smart."

- Logical-mathematical strengths include math aptitude, interest in science, problem solving skills, and logical thinking. People with this intelligence are "number/reasoning smart."

- Spatial strengths include visualization, understanding puzzles, navigation, visual arts, reading, and writing. People with this intelligence are "picture smart."

- Bodily-kinesthetic strengths include hand and eye coordination, athletics, dance, drama, cooking, sculpting, and learning by doing. People with this intelligence are "body smart."

- Linguistic strengths include good reading, writing, vocabulary, and spelling skills; good communication skills; being a good listener; having a good memory, and learning new languages easily. People with this intelligence are "word smart."

© 2013, SHUTTERSTOCK, INC.

- Intrapersonal strengths include good self-awareness. They are aware of their feelings and emotions and are often independent and self-motivated to achieve. People with this intelligence are "self-smart."
- Naturalist strengths include exploring and preserving the environment and are very aware of natural surroundings. People with this intelligence are "nature smart."
- Existential strengths include reflecting on important questions about the universe, the purpose of life, and religious beliefs. People with this intelligence are "curiosity smart."

Activity

In what areas are you "smart?"

_____

_____

_____

_____

_____

Some Careers and Multiple Intelligences

Circle any careers that seem interesting to you.

Musical	Interpersonal	Logical-Mathematical
Disc Jockey	Cruise Director	Engineer
Music Teacher	Mediator	Accountant
Music Retailer	Human Resources	Computer Analyst
Music Therapist	Dental Hygienist	Physician
Recording Engineer	Nurse	Detective
Singer	Psychologist	Researcher
Song Writer	Social Worker	Scientist
Speech Pathologist	Administrator	Computer Programmer
Music Librarian	Marketer	Database Designer
Choir Director	Religious Leader	Physicist
Music Critic	Teacher	Auditor
Music Lawyer	Counselor	Economist

Spatial	Bodily-Kinesthetic	Linguistic
Architect	Athlete	Journalist
Artist	Carpenter	Writer
Film Animator	Craftsperson	Editor
Mechanic	Mechanic	Attorney
Pilot	Jeweler	Curator
Webmaster	Computer Game Designer	Newscaster
Interior Decorator	Firefighter	Politician
Graphic Artist	Forest Ranger	Speech Pathologist
Sculptor	Physical Therapist	Translator
Surveyor	Personal Trainer	Comedian
Urban Planner	Surgeon	Historian
Photographer	Recreation Specialist	Librarian
		Marketing Consultant

Intrapersonal	Naturalist	Existential
Career Counselor	Park Ranger	Counselor
Wellness Counselor	Dog Trainer	Psychologist
Therapist	Landscaper	Psychiatrist
Criminologist	Meteorologist	Social Worker
intelligence Officer	Veterinarian	Ministry
Entrepreneur	Animal Health Technician	Philosopher
Psychologist	Ecologist	Artist
Researcher	Nature Photographer	Scientist
Actor	Wilderness Guide	Researcher
Artist	Anthropologist	Motivational Speaker
Philosopher	Environmental Lawyer	Human Resources
Writer	Water Conservationist	Writer

"The best years of your life are the ones in which you decide your problems are your own. You do not blame them on your mother, the ecology, or the president. You realize that you control your own destiny."

ALBERT ELLIS

Quiz

Multiple Intelligences

Test what you have learned by selecting the correct answers to the following questions.

1. Multiple intelligences are defined as
   a. the many parts of intelligence as measured by an IQ test.
   b. the ability to design something valued in at least one culture.
   c. the ability to read, write, and do mathematical computations.

2. The concept of multiple intelligences is significant because
   a. it measures the intelligence of students in schools.
   b. it does not use culture in measuring intelligence.
   c. it broadens the scope of human potential and includes all cultures.

3. Intelligences are measured by
   a. IQ tests.
   b. performance in activities related to the intelligence.
   c. performance in the classroom.

4. Each individual's life history contains crystallizers that
   a. promote the development of the intelligences.
   b. inhibit the development of the intelligences.
   c. cause the individual to be set in their ways.

5. Multiple intelligences include
   a. getting good grades in college.
   b. bodily kinesthetic skills.
   c. good test-taking skills.

How did you do on the quiz? Check your answers: 1. b, 2. c, 3. b, 4. a, 5. b

Using Emotional Intelligence

Emotional intelligence is related to interpersonal and intrapersonal intelligences. It is the ability to recognize, control, and evaluate your own emotions while realizing how they affect people around you. Emotional intelligence affects career success, because it is related to our ability to express ourselves, work as part of a team, concentrate, remember, make decisions, deal with stress, overcome challenges, deal with conflict, and empathize with others. Research has shown emotional intelligence can predict career success and that workers with high emotional intelligence are more likely to end up in leadership positions in which they are happy with their jobs.[3]

The premise of emotional intelligence is that you can be more successful if you are aware of your own emotions as well as the emotions of others. There are two aspects of emotional intelligence:

• Understanding yourself, your goals, intentions, responses, and behavior.
• Understanding others and their feelings.

Daniel Goleman has identified the five most important characteristics of emotional intelligence:[4]

1. **Self-Awareness.** People with high emotional intelligence are aware of their emotions, including strengths and weaknesses.

2. **Self-Regulation.** This involves the ability to control emotions and impulses. Being impulsive can lead to careless decisions like attending a party the night before a final exam. Characteristics of self-regulation include comfort with change, integrity, and the ability to say no.

3. **Motivation.** People with high emotional intelligence can defer immediate results for long-term success. For example, investing your time in education can lead to future career opportunities and income.

4. **Empathy.** Empathy is the ability to understand the needs and viewpoints of others around you and avoiding stereotypes. It involves good listening skills that enhance personal relationships.

5. **Social Skills.** People with good social skills are good team players and willing to help others to be successful.

   You can enhance your career success by developing your emotional intelligence. Here are some tips for improving your emotional intelligence and managing personal relationships on the job.

- Be empathetic when working with others by trying to put yourself in their place to understand different perspectives and points of view. Don't be quick to jump to conclusions or stereotype others.
- Think about how your actions affect others. Always treat others as you would like to be treated.
- Be open-minded and intellectually curious. Consider the opinions of others in a positive manner. Be willing to examine and change your mindset.
- Give others credit for their accomplishments in the workplace. When speaking about your own accomplishments, confidently state what you did without trying to seek too much attention.
- Evaluate your own strengths and weaknesses. Focus on your strengths, but be aware of the weaknesses and work to improve them. The personality assessment in Chapter 2 helps you to understand your personal strengths and weaknesses.
- Work on stress management by finding some stress reduction techniques that work for you. In stressful situations, it is helpful to remain calm and in control. Seek workable solutions without blaming others. Your college health services office often provides workshops on stress management.
- Take a college course to improve verbal as well as nonverbal communication. When talking with others, focus on what they are saying rather than what you are going to say next. Learn how to make "I statements" that effectively communicate your thoughts without blaming others. Become aware of nonverbal communication, which adds a significant dimension to communication.
- Use humor to help you deal with challenges. Humor helps you to keep things in perspective, deal with differences, relax, and come up with creative solutions.
- Deal with conflicts in a way that builds trust. Focus on win-win solutions that allow both parties to have their needs met.
- Take responsibility for your actions. Admit when you make mistakes and work to improve the situation in the future.
- Use critical thinking to analyze the pros and cons of the situation.
- Be goal oriented and focus on the task and the steps needed to achieve your goals.
- Be optimistic. Optimism leads to greater opportunities and results in better personal relationships.

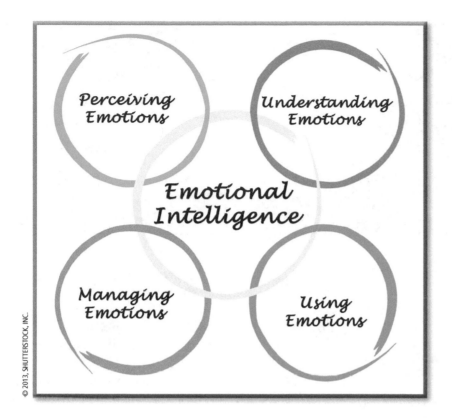

© 2013, SHUTTERSTOCK, INC.

© 2013, SHUTTERSTOCK, INC.

Journal
Entry

Comment on your emotional intelligence and how you can use it to be successful in your career.

3

What Are My Lifetime Goals?

You have now completed the assessment part of the course and have a greater awareness of your personal strengths, vocational interests, values, and multiple intelligences. Use this knowledge to begin thinking about some goals for the future.

Setting goals helps you to establish what is important and provides direction for your life. Goals help you to focus your energy on what you want to accomplish. Goals are a promise to yourself to improve your life. Setting goals can help you turn your dreams into reality. Steven Scott in his book, *A Millionaire's Notebook,* lays out five steps in this process:

1. Dream or visualize.

2. Convert the dream into goals.

3. Convert your goals into tasks.

4. Convert your task into steps.

5. Take your first step and then the next.[5]

As you begin to think about your personal goals in life, make your goals specific and concrete. Rather than saying, "I want to be rich," make your goal something that you can break into specific steps. You might want to start learning about money management or begin a savings plan. Rather than setting a goal for happiness, think about

"A goal is a dream with a deadline."

NAPOLEON HILL

what brings you happiness. If you want to live a long and healthy life, think about the health habits that will help you to accomplish your goal. You will need to break your goals down into specific tasks to be able to accomplish them.

Here are some criteria for successful goal setting:

1. **Is it achievable?** Do I have the skills, abilities, and resources to accomplish this goal? If not, am I willing to spend the time to develop the skills, abilities, and resources needed to achieve this goal?

2. **Is it realistic?** Do I believe I can achieve it? Am I positive and optimistic about this goal?

3. **Is it specific and measurable?** Can it be counted or observed? The most common goal mentioned by students is happiness in life. What is happiness, and how will you know when you have achieved it? Is happiness a career you enjoy, owning your own home, or a travel destination?

4. **Do you want to do it?** Is this a goal you are choosing because it gives you personal satisfaction rather than meeting a requirement or an expectation of someone else?

5. **Are you motivated to achieve it?** What are your rewards for achieving it?

6. **Does the goal match your values?** Is it important to you?

7. **What steps do you need to take to begin?** Am I willing to take action to start working on it?

8. **When will you finish this goal?** Set a date to accomplish your goal.

Journal Entry

Write a paragraph about your lifetime goals. Use any of these questions to guide your thinking:

What is your career goal? If you do not know what your career goal is, describe your preferred work environment. Would your ideal career require a college degree?

What are your family goals? Are you interested in marriage and family? What would be your important family values?

What are your social goals (friends, community, and recreation)?

When you are older and look back on your life, what are the three most important life goals that you would want to make sure to accomplish?

A Goal or a Fantasy?

One of the best questions ever asked in my class was, "What is the difference between a goal and a fantasy?" As you look at your list of lifetime goals, are some of these items goals or fantasies? Think about this question as you read the following scenario:

© 2013, SHUTTERSTOCK, INC.

When Linda was a college student, she was walking through the parking lot and noticed a beautiful red sports car and decided that it would become a lifetime goal to own a similar car one day. However, with college expenses and her part-time job, it was not possible to buy the car. She would have to be content with the used car that her dad had given her so that she could drive to college. Years passed by, and Linda now has a good job, a home, and a family. She is reading a magazine and sees a picture of a similar red sports car. She cuts out this picture and tapes it to the refrigerator. After it has been on the refrigerator for several months, her children ask her why the picture is on the refrigerator. Linda replies, "I just like to dream about owning this car." One day as Linda is driving past a car dealership, she sees the red sports car on display and stops in for a test drive. To her surprise, she decides that she does not like driving the car. It doesn't fit her lifestyle either. She enjoys outdoor activities that would require a larger car. Buying a second car would be costly and reduce the amount of money that the family could spend on vacations. She decides that vacations are more important than owning the sports car. Linda goes home and removes the picture of the red sports car from the refrigerator.

> "Vision without action is a daydream. Action without vision is a nightmare."
> JAPANESE PROVERB

There are many differences between a goal and a fantasy. A fantasy is a dream that may or may not become a reality. A goal is something that we actually plan to achieve. Sometimes we begin with a fantasy and later it becomes a goal. A fantasy can become a goal if steps are taken to achieve it. In the preceding example, the sports car is a fantasy until Linda actually takes the car for a test drive. After driving the car, she decides that she really does not want it. The fantasy is sometimes better than the reality. Goals and fantasies change over a lifetime. We set goals, try them out, and

> "In life, as in football, you won't go far unless you know where the goalposts are."
> ARNOLD GLASGOW

change them as we grow and mature and find out what is most important in life. Knowing what we think is important, and what we value most, helps us make good decisions about lifetime goals.

What is the difference between a goal and a fantasy? A goal is something that requires action. Ask yourself if you are willing to take action on the goals you have set for yourself. Begin to take action by thinking about the steps needed to accomplish the goal. Then take the first step and continue. Change your goals if they are no longer important to you.

Quiz

Emotional Intelligence and Goal Setting

1. Emotional intelligence involves

   a. self-criticism.
   b. self-awareness.
   c. self-doubt.

2. A criteria for successful goal setting includes

   a. is it achievable?
   b. can you postpone it?
   c. is it worth your time?

3. An important step in goal setting is

   a. getting started when you feel like it.
   b. asking others what is important.
   c. identifying the steps needed to get started.

4. An example of a measurable goal is:

   a. I will be rich.
   b. I will be financially secure.
   c. I will open a savings account.

5. The difference between a goal and a fantasy is

   _____.

   a. action
   b. money
   c. luck

How did you do on the quiz? Check your answers: 1. b, 2. a, 3. c, 4. c, 5. a

© 2013, SHUTTERSTOCK, INC.

Keys to Success
Create Your Future

We are responsible for what happens in our lives. We make decisions and choices that create the future. Our behavior leads to success or failure. Too often we believe that we are victims of circumstance. When looking at our lives, we often look for others to blame for how our life is going:

- My grandparents did it to me. I inherited these genes.
- My parents did it to me. My childhood experiences shaped who I am.
- My teacher did it to me. He gave me a poor grade.
- My boss did it to me. She gave me a poor evaluation.
- The government did it to me. All my money goes to taxes.
- Society did it to me. I have no opportunity.

These factors are powerful influences in our lives, but we are still left with choices. Concentration camp survivor Viktor Frankl wrote a book, *Man's Search for Meaning*, in which he describes his experiences and how he survived his ordeal. His parents, brother, and wife died in the camps. He suffered starvation and torture. Through all of his sufferings and imprisonment, he still maintained that he was a free man because he could make choices.

We who lived in concentration camps can remember the men who walked through the huts comforting others, giving away their last piece of bread. They may have been few in number, but they offer sufficient proof that everything can be taken from a man but one thing: the last of the human freedoms—to choose one's attitude in any given set of circumstances, to choose one's own way. . . . Fundamentally, therefore, any man can, even under such circumstances, decide what shall become of him—mentally and spiritually. He may retain his human dignity even in a concentration camp.[6]

Viktor Frankl could not choose his circumstances at that time, but he did choose his attitude. He decided how he would respond to the situation. He realized that he still had the freedom to make choices. He used his memory and imagination to exercise his freedom. When times were the most difficult, he would imagine that he was in the classroom lecturing to his students about psychology. He eventually did get out of the concentration camp and became a famous psychiatrist.

Hopefully none of you will ever have to experience the circumstances faced by Viktor Frankl, but we all face challenging situations. It is empowering to think that our behavior is more a function of our decisions rather than our circumstances. It is not productive to look around and find someone to blame for your problems. Psychologist Abraham Maslow says that instead of blaming we should see how we can make the best of the situation.

One can spend a lifetime assigning blame, finding a cause, "out there" for all the troubles that exist. Contrast this with the responsible attitude of confronting the situation, bad or good, and instead of asking, "What caused the trouble? Who was to blame?", asking, "How can I handle the present situation to make the best of it?"[7]

Author Stephen Covey suggests that we look at the word responsibility as "response-ability."[8] It is the ability to choose responses and make decisions about the future. When you are dealing with a problem, it is useful to ask yourself what decisions you made that led to the problem. How did you create the situation? If you created the problem, you can create a solution.

At times, you may ask, "How did I create this?", and find that the answer is that you did not create the situation. We certainly do not create earthquakes or hurricanes, for example. But we do create or at least contribute to many of the things that happen to us. Even if you did not create your circumstances, you can create your reaction to the situation. In the case of an earthquake, you can decide to panic or find the best course of action at the moment.

Stephen Covey believes that we can use our resourcefulness and initiative in dealing with most problems. When his children were growing up and they asked him how to solve a certain problem, he would say, "Use your R and I!". He meant resourcefulness and initiative. He notes that adults can use this R and I to get a good job.

But the people who end up with the good jobs are the proactive ones who are solutions to problems, not problems themselves, who seize the initiative to do whatever is necessary, consistent with correct principles, to get the job done.[9]

Use your resourcefulness and initiative to create the future that you want.

Journal
Entry
How can you create the future you want for yourself?

5

JOURNALENTRIES

EXPLORING YOUR MULTIPLE INTELLIGENCES

Go to http://www.collegesuccess1.com/JournalEntries.htm for Word files of the Journal Entries.

SUCCESS
over the Internet

Visit the *College Success Website* at http://www.collegesuccess1.com/

The *College Success Website* is continually updated with new topics and links to the material presented in this chapter. Topics include:

- Multiple intelligences
- Emotional intelligence
- Goal setting

Contact your instructor if you have any problems in accessing the *College Success Website.*

Notes

1. Howard Gardner, *Intelligence Reframed: Multiple Intelligences for the Twenty-First Century* (Boulder, CO: Basic Books, 1999).
2. Thomas Armstrong, *Multiple Intelligences in the Classroom* (Alexandria, VA: Association for Curriculum Development, 1994).
3. "Emotional Intelligence in Career Planning," accessed August 2013, https://www1.cfnc.org/
4. "Emotional Intelligence, Developing Strong People Skills," accessed August 2013, http://www.mindtools.com/pages/article/newCDV_59.htm
5. Steven K. Scott, *A Millionaire's Notebook*, quoted in Rob Gilbert, Editor, *Bits & Pieces*, November 4, 1999, p. 15.
6. Viktor Frankl, *Man's Search for Meaning* (New York: Pocket Books, 1963), 104–105.
7. Quoted in Rob Gilbert, ed., *Bits and Pieces,* November 4, 1999.
8. Stephen Covey, *The 7 Habits of Highly Effective People* (New York: Simon and Schuster, 1989), 71.
9. Ibid., 75.

MY LIFETIME GOALS: BRAINSTORMING ACTIVITY

1. Think about the goals that you would like to accomplish in your life. At the end of your life, you do not want to say, "I wish I would have _____." Set a timer for five minutes and write whatever comes to mind about what you would like to do and accomplish over your lifetime. Include goals in these areas: career, personal relationships, travel, and financial security, or any area that is important to you. Write down all your ideas. The goal is to generate as many ideas as possible in five minutes. You can reflect on which ones are most important later. You may want to do this as part of a group activity in your class.

Look over the ideas you wrote above and highlight or underline the goals that are most important to you.

2. Ask yourself what you would like to accomplish in the next five years. Think about where you want to be in college, what you want to do in your career, and what you want to do in your personal life. Set a timer and write whatever comes to mind in five minutes. The goal is to write down as many ideas as possible.

Again, look over the ideas you wrote and highlight or underline the ideas that are most important to you.

3. What goals would you like to accomplish in the next year? What are some steps that you can begin now to accomplish your lifetime goals? Consider work, study, leisure, and social goals. Set your timer for five minutes and write down your goals for the next year.

Review what you wrote and highlight or underline the ideas that are most important to you. When writing your goals, include fun activities as well as taking care of others.

Looking at the items that you have highlighted or underlined, make a list of your lifetime goals using the form that follows. Make sure your goals are specific enough so that you can break them into steps you can achieve.

MY LIFETIME GOALS

Using the ideas that you brainstormed in the previous exercise, make a list of your lifetime goals. Make sure your goals are specific and concrete. Begin with goals that you would like to accomplish over a lifetime. In the second section, think about the goals you can accomplish over the next one to three years.

Long-Term Goals (lifetime goals)

Short-Term Goals (one to three years)

What are some steps you can take now to accomplish intermediate and long-term goals?

SUCCESSFUL GOAL SETTING

Look at your list of lifetime goals. Which one is most important? Write the goal here:

Answer these questions about the goal you have listed above.

1. What skills, abilities, and resources do you have to achieve this goal? What skills, abilities, and resources will you need to develop to achieve this goal?

2. Do you believe you can achieve it? Write a brief positive statement about achieving this goal.

3. State your goal in specific terms that can be observed or counted. Rewrite your goal if necessary.

4. Write a brief statement about how this goal will give you personal satisfaction.

5. How will you motivate yourself to achieve this goal?

6. What are your personal values that match this goal?

7. List some steps that you will take to accomplish this goal.

8. When will you finish this goal?

9. What roadblocks will make this goal difficult to achieve?

10. How will you deal with these roadblocks?

Planning Your Career and Education

5

Learning
OBJECTIVES

Read to answer these key questions:

- What are some employment trends for the future?

- What are work skills necessary for success in the twenty-first century?

- How do I research a career?

- How do I plan my education?

- How can I make good decisions about my future?

- What is a dangerous opportunity?

It is always easier to get where you are going if you have a road map or a plan. To start the journey, it is helpful to know about yourself, including your personality, interests, talents, and values. Once you have this picture, you will need to know about the world of work and job trends that will affect your future employment opportunities. Next, you will need to make decisions about which road to follow. Then, you will need to plan your education to reach your destination.

Employment Trends

The world is changing quickly, and these changes will affect your future career. To assure your future career success, you will need to become aware of career trends and observe how they change over time so that you can adjust your career plans accordingly. For example, recently a school was established for training bank tellers. The school quickly went out of business and the students demanded their money back because they were not able to get jobs. A careful observer of career trends would have noticed that bank tellers are being replaced by automatic teller machines (ATMs) and would not have started a school for training bank tellers. Students observant of career trends would not have paid money for the training. It is probably a good idea for bank tellers to look ahead and plan a new career direction.

How can you find out about career trends that may affect you in the future? Become a careful observer by reading about current events. Good sources of information include:

- Your local newspaper, especially the business section
- News programs
- Current magazines
- Government statistics and publications
- The Internet

When thinking about future trends, use your critical thinking skills. Sometimes trends change quickly or interact in different ways. For example, since we are using email to a great extent today, it might seem that mail carriers would not be as much in demand in the future. However, since people are buying more goods over the Internet, there has been an increased demand for mail carriers and other delivery services. Develop the habit of looking at what is happening to see if you can identify trends that may affect your future.

Usually trends get started as a way to meet the following needs:[1]

- To save money
- To reduce cost
- To do things faster
- To make things easier to use
- To improve safety and reliability
- To lessen the impact on the environment

The following are some trends to watch that may affect your future career. As you read about each trend, think about how it could affect you.

Baby Boomers, Generation X, the Millennials, and the New Generation Z

About every 20 years, sociologists begin to describe a new generation with similar characteristics based on shared historical experiences. Each generation has different opportunities and challenges in the workplace.

The Baby Boomers were born following World War II between 1946 and 1964. Four out of every 10 adults today are in this Baby Boom Generation.[2] Because there are so many aging Baby Boomers, the average age of Americans is increasing. Life expectancy is also increasing. By 2015 the projected life expectancy will be 76.4 for men and 81.4 for women.[3] In the new millennium, many more people will live to be 100 years old or more! Think about the implications of an older population. Older people need such things as health care, recreation, travel, and financial planning. Occupations related to these needs are likely to be in demand now and in the future.

Those born between 1965 and 1977 are often referred to as Generation X. They are sometimes called the "baby bust" generation because fewer babies were born during this period than in the previous generations. There is much in the media about this generation having to pay higher taxes and Social Security payments to support the large number of aging Baby Boomers. Some say that this generation will not enjoy the prosperity of the Baby Boomers. Those who left college in the early nineties faced a recession and the worst job market since World War II.[4] Many left college in debt and returned home to live with their parents. Because of a lack of employment opportunities, many in this generation became entrepreneurs, starting new companies at a faster rate than previous generations.

Jane Bryant Quinn notes that in spite of economic challenges, Generation Xers have a lot going for them:[5]

- They have record-high levels of education, which correlate with higher income and lower unemployment.
- There is a demand for more skilled workers, so employers are more willing to train employees. Anthony Carnevale, chairman of the National Commission for Employment Policy, "sees a big demand for 'high-school plus'—a high school diploma plus technical school or junior college."
- Generation Xers are computer literate, and those who use computers on the job earn 10 to 15 percent more than those who don't.
- This group often has a good work ethic valued by employers. However, they value a balanced lifestyle with time for outside interests and family.
- As Baby Boomers retire, more job opportunities are created for this group.
- Unlike the Baby Boomers, this generation was born into a more integrated and more diverse society. They are better able than previous generations to adapt to diversity in society and the workplace.

Many of today's college students are part of the Millennial Generation, born between 1977 and 1995. This generation is sometimes called Generation Y or the Echo Boomers, since they are the children of the Baby Boomers.[6] This new generation of approximately 60 million is three times larger than Generation X and will eventually exceed the number of Baby Boomers. In this decade, they will become the largest teen population in U.S. history. As the Millennials reach college age, they will attend college in increasing numbers. In the next 10 years, college enrollments will increase by approximately 300,000 students per year. Colleges will find it difficult to accommodate rapidly increasing numbers of students, and as a result, the Millennial Generation will face increasingly competitive college admissions criteria.

Millennials are more ethnically diverse than previous generations with 34 percent ethnic minorities. One in four lives with a single parent; three in four have working mothers. Most of them started using computers before they were five years old. Marketing researchers describe this new generation as "technologically adept, info-savvy, a cyber-generation, the clickeratti."[7] They are the connected generation, accustomed to cell phones, chatting on the Internet, and listening to downloaded music.

Young people in the Millennial Generation share a different historical perspective from the Baby Boom Generation. Baby Boomers remember the Vietnam War and the assassinations of President John F. Kennedy and Martin Luther King. For Millennials, school shootings such as Columbine and acts of terrorism such as the Oklahoma City bombing and the 9–11 attack on New York City stand out as important events. The Millennial Generation will see their main problems as dealing with violence, easy access to weapons, and the threat of terrorism.

Neil Howe and William Strauss paint a very positive picture of this new generation in their book *Millennials Rising: The Next Great Generation*:

- Millennials will rebel by tearing down old institutions that do not work and building new and better institutions. The authors predict that this will be the can-do generation filled with technology planners, community shapers, institution builders, and world leaders.
- Surveys show that this generation describes themselves as happy, confident, and positive.
- They are cooperative team players.
- They generally accept authority and respect their parents' values.
- They follow rules. The rates of homicides, violent crime, abortion, and teen pregnancy are decreasing rapidly.
- The use of alcohol, drugs, and tobacco is decreasing.
- Millennials have a fascination with and mastery of new technology.
- Their most important values are individuality and uniqueness.[8]

In the past, new generations emerged about every 20 years. However, because of rapid social change, generations are now being defined in shorter time periods. A new generation born since 1995 is currently emerging. Various names for this generation have been proposed, such as Generation Z, Generation Wii, the iGeneration, Gen Tech, Digital Natives, Net Gen, and the Plurals.[9] These names reflect this generation's fascination with and ease of using technology as well as their increasing diversity. This is a large generation, with one in four Americans under 18 years old.[10]

This generation has been affected by historical events such as the election of President Obama (the first biracial president), events surrounding 9/11, wars in Iraq and Afghanistan, the tsunami and nuclear meltdown in Japan, school violence, and economic recession. They are referred to as digital natives since they have always lived in a world with the Internet, cell phones and iPods, and other devices.

Some characteristics of this new generation include:[11]

- This is the last generation with a Caucasian majority. Only 55 percent of this generation is Caucasian as compared to 72 percent of Baby Boomers. In 2019, less than 50 percent of births will be Caucasian.
- They are more positive than older Americans about becoming an ethnically diverse society and more likely to have friends from different racial, ethnic, and religious groups.

- There is a continuing decline in two-parent households with only two out of three people from two-parent households. Increased same-sex marriage is changing the definition of family.

- Because of the extended recession, they are less likely to believe in the "American Dream" and to be hopeful for the future. They tend to be more realistic.

- Women are more likely to get a college degree and they hold 51 percent of managerial and professional jobs. As a result, gender roles are blending, with men assuming more familial responsibilities

- It is an age of "girl power." Girls between the ages of 8–15 care more about their grades than boys and have more expectations of receiving a college degree and having work that changes the world.

- Technology will continue to influence this group as in the New Millennial Generation. Use of technology will transform the way that people communicate and purchase goods. People will communicate with shorter and more immediate communications such as texting and Twitter. More purchases will be made on the Internet.

- This generation hopes to use technology as a tool to change the world.

It is predicted that the world of work for the Millennials and Generation Z will be dramatically different. Previous generations anticipated having a lifetime career. By the year 2020, many jobs will probably be short-term contracts. This arrangement will provide cost savings and efficiency for employers and flexibility for employees to start or stop work to take vacations, train for new jobs, or meet family responsibilities. One in five people will be self-employed. Retirement will be postponed as people look forward to living longer and healthier lives.[12]

Journal
Entry

> Describe your generation (Baby Boomer, Generation X, New Millennial, or Generation Z). What are your best qualities and challenges?

1

Moving from Goods to Services and Technology

Human society has moved through several stages. The first stage, about 20,000 years ago, was the hunting and gathering stage. During this time, society depended on the natural environment for food and other resources. When natural resources were depleted, the community moved to another area. The second stage, some 10,000 years ago, was the agricultural stage. Human beings learned to domesticate animals and cultivate crops. This allowed people to stay in one place and develop more permanent villages. About 200 years ago, industrial societies came into being by harnessing power sources to produce goods on a large scale.

Today in the United States, we are evolving into a service, technology, and information society. Fewer people are working in agriculture and manufacturing. Futurists John Naisbitt et al. note that we are moving toward a service economy based on high technology, rapid communications, biotechnology for use in agriculture and medicine, health care, and sales of merchandise.[13] Service areas with increasing numbers of jobs include health care and social assistance; professional, scientific, and technical services; educational services; administrative and support services; waste management and remediation services; accommodation and food services; government; retail trade; transportation and warehousing, finance and insurance; arts, entertainment, and recreation; wholesale trade; real estate, rental, and leasing; and information and management.

Increased Opportunities in Health Care

If you are interested in science and technology along with helping other people, there are many career opportunities in health care. It is estimated that by 2018, there will be an increase of four million new jobs in health care, which will account for 26 percent of all new jobs.[14] This trend is being driven by an aging population, increased longevity, health care reform, and new developments in the pharmaceutical and medical fields. Because of increased health care costs, many of the jobs done by doctors, nurses, dentists, or physical therapists are now being done by physician's assistants, medical assistants, dental assistants, physical therapy aides, and home health aides. Health care workers will increasingly use technology to do their work. For example, a new occupation is nursing informatics, which combines traditional nursing skills with computer and information science.

Increased Need for Education

In the past, the life pattern for many people was to graduate from school, go to work, and eventually retire. Because of the rapid changes in technology and society today, workers will need additional training and education over a lifetime. Education will take place in a variety of forms: community college courses, training on the job, private training sessions, and learning on your own. Those who do not keep up with the new technology will find that their skills quickly become obsolete. Those who do keep up will find their skills in demand.

As we transition from manufacturing to service and technical careers, education beyond high school will become increasingly important. According to the Bureau of Labor Statistics, occupations that require a postsecondary degree will account for nearly half of all new jobs from 2008 to 2018, with the fastest growth in jobs requiring an associate's degree or higher. In addition, higher education will result in higher earnings and lower unemployment.[15]

Young people who do not continue their education are likely to be stuck in lower-paying jobs, while those who continue their education will have higher-paying jobs.

FIGURE 5.1 Projected percent increase in employment, 2008 through 2018.[16]

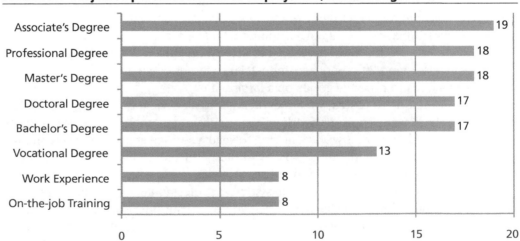

Author Joyce Lain Kennedy believes that the middle class is becoming an endangered species.[17] She states that many jobs traditionally held by the middle class have been "dumbed down," making them so simple that anyone can do them. These jobs pay very little and offer no benefits, no employment stability, and little opportunity for advancement. Young people often hold these jobs in their teens and twenties.

At the other end of the job continuum are jobs requiring a college education or training beyond high school. These high-end jobs often require technical or computer skills. These are the jobs that pay better and offer benefits. It seems that we are becoming a nation of haves and have-nots who are separated by their education and technical skills.

Going Green!

Have you purchased organic products or an energy-efficient light bulb, appliance, or car? If so, you are part of a new environmental movement that is gaining impetus in the U.S., the rise of social responsibility and the citizen consumer. Businesses that are seen as green attract consumers who are concerned about using energy efficiently, new sources of energy, and preserving the environment. In addition to profit, businesses are now concerned about the planet and working conditions for people.

As fossil fuels are depleted, the world is facing a major transformation in how energy is generated and used. Sustainability, wind turbines, solar panels, farmer's markets, biofuels, and wind energy are just some of the ways to transition to a post-fossil-fuel world. Jobs in this field will include engineers who design new technology, consultants to audit energy needs, and installers who install and maintain systems. Here are some titles of green jobs: environmental lawyer, environmental technician, sustainability consultant, sustainability project director, green architect, green building project manager, marine biologist, environmental technician, energy efficiency specialist, organic farmer, compliance manager, product engineer, wind energy engineer, and solar engineer.

A Diverse Workforce

The workforce in the United States is becoming increasingly more diverse. Diversity includes many demographic variables such as ethnicity, religion, gender, national origin, disability, sexual orientation, age, education, geographic origin, and skill characteristics. Having an appreciation for diversity is important in maintaining a work environment that is open and allows for individual differences. Increasing diversity provides opportunities for many different kinds of individuals and makes it important to be able to have good working relationships with all kinds of people.

The U.S. Bureau of Labor Statistics has described some trends that will affect the workplace by 2018.[18]

- Whites are expected to make up a decreasing share of the labor force, while Blacks, Asians, and all other groups will increase their share. Persons of Hispanic origin will increase their share of the labor force from 14.3 to 17.6 percent, reflecting a 33.1 percent growth.
- The number of women in the labor force will grow at a slightly faster rate than the number of men. The male labor force is projected to grow by 7.5 percent, as compared with 9.0 percent for the female labor force.
- The number of workers in younger age groups will decline, while workers in the 55 years and older group will increase, reflecting the increase of aging Baby Boomers.
- Total employment is expected to increase by 10 percent from 2008 to 2018. Changes in consumer demand and advances in technology will continue to change the structure of the economy, with decreasing jobs in manufacturing and increasing numbers of jobs in service and technology.

E-Commerce Is Changing the Way We Do Business

E-commerce, the purchasing of goods, services, and information over the Internet, is a new technology that has revolutionized the way business is done in the 21st century. More people are using e-commerce because of convenience, selection, and the ease of shopping for goods at the best price. Online sales are a growing part of the market, increasing 10 to 20 percent a year for the last several years. By 2017, the Web will account for 10 percent of retail sales. An additional 43 percent of sales will be influenced by online research.[19] This growth in e-commerce will have implications for education and business. More colleges are offering courses in e-commerce and incorporating e-commerce topics into traditional business offerings. There are more career opportunities in e-commerce and related fields such as computer graphics, web design, online marketing, and package delivery services.

The Microprocessor

The microprocessor is a silicon chip containing transistors that determine the capability of a computer. In the past 20 years, the power of the microprocessor has increased more than one million times. In the next 20 years, the power will increase a million times again.[20] Because of the increased power of the microprocessor, it will be used in new ways and with new devices. Consider the "smart home" of the future:

> As you reach the front door, you are welcomed by a flat screen, rather than a doorbell. You can use this screen to ring the doorbell, talk to the person inside the home or leave a message, which can be accessed by telephone or e-mail.
>
> If you're the homeowner, walk through the door and the curtains go up, letting light in, and the entire house is soon subtly illuminated. The hi-fi will access its database to play your favorite music, and the air-conditioning will be preset to the temperature you prefer.
>
> As you move to the kitchen, you take the ingredients for your lunch—say, flour, a piece of fish and a few stalks of broccoli—to a networked table. This will activate a system that will immediately offer you a range of appropriate recipes. Your smart microwave will fix the dish for you, consulting the recipe you prefer, via the Internet.[21]

The microprocessor is increasingly available to all and for less cost. The personal computer would have occupied an entire building 35 years ago. Today we have access to powerful computers and mobile devices that will play an ever greater role in our daily lives.

> *It's remarkable how we now take all that power for granted. Using a basic home PC costing less than $1,000, you can balance your household budget, do your taxes, write letters to friends and fax or e-mail them over the Internet, listen to CDs or the radio, watch the news, consult a doctor, play games, book a vacation, view a house, buy a book or a car. The list is endless.[22]*

New Advances in Technology and Communication

There has been a recent rapid increase in the development of cell phones and other mobile devices, as well as the use of social media, which will continue to have a major impact on career opportunities. Those who can keep up with the current technology will find increasing career and business opportunities. Graduates will become more marketable if they combine traditional career areas with technology such as social media. For example, students in a marketing degree program will be more in demand if they can use Facebook, LinkedIn, or Twitter to market products.

The Bureau of Labor Statistics reports that two million technology-related jobs will be created by 2018. Jobs in computer systems design and related services are expected to increase by 34 percent by 2018. Jobs that will grow faster than the average include computer-network administrators, data-communications analysts, and Web developers. Some new fields include data-loss prevention, online security, and risk management. Computer science degrees are especially marketable when combined with traditional majors such as finance, accounting, or marketing.[23]

Because we are living in the Information Age, information and technology workers are now the largest group of workers in the United States. Careers in information technology include the design, development, and support of computer software, hardware, and networks. Some newer jobs in this area include animation for video

games, films, and videos as well as setting up websites and Internet security. There are also good opportunities for network programmers who can program a group of computers to work together. Because computer use has increased greatly, it is expected that computer-related jobs will expand by 40 percent or more in the next decade.[24]

In the future, computers will continue to become more powerful, mobile, and connected. It is predicted that by 2018, microprocessors will be replaced by optical computers that function at the speed of light. Technology will be embedded in products used for entertainment as well as for home and business use. It is predicted that in the future, the desktop computer as we know it will cease to exist. Instead of a home computer, we will have computerized homes with sensors that monitor energy use and smart appliances with computer chips. Gestures, touch, and voice communication will rapidly replace computer keyboards. The Nintendo Wii™ and the iPhone are current examples. Computers will move from homes and offices into human bodies. Microchips may be embedded in human bodies to monitor health conditions and to deliver medical care. Some futurists forecast a time when computer chips will be embedded in the brain and connected to the Internet. Of course, computer security will become increasingly important with these new advances.[25]

Radiation and laser technologies will provide new technical careers in the future. It has been said that lasers will be as important to the 21st century as electricity was for the 20th century. New uses for lasers are being found in medicine, energy, industry, computers, communications, entertainment, and outer space. The use of lasers is creating new jobs and causing others to become obsolete. For example, many welders are being replaced by laser technicians, who have significantly higher earnings. New jobs will open for people who purchase, install, and maintain lasers.

Careers in fiber optics and telecommunications are among the top new emerging fields in the 21st century. Fiber optics are thin glass fibers that transmit light. This new technology may soon make copper wire obsolete. One of the most important uses of fiber optics is to speed up delivery of data over the Internet and to improve telecommunications. It is also widely used in medical instruments, including laser surgery.

Another interesting development to watch is artificial intelligence software, which enables computers to recognize patterns, improve from experience, make inferences, and approximate human thought. Scientists at the MIT Artificial Intelligence Lab have developed a robot named Cog. Here is a description of Cog and its capabilities:

> We have given it a multitude of sensors to "feel" and learn what it is like to be touched and spoken to. Cog's ability to make eye contact and reach out to moving objects is also meant to motivate people to interact with it. These features have taught Cog, among other things, to distinguish a human face from inanimate objects (this puts its development at about a 3-month-old's). It can also listen to music and keep rhythm by tapping on a drum (something a 5-year-old can do). One of the most startling moments in Cog's development came when it was learning to touch things. At one point, Cog began to touch and discover its own body. It looked so eerie and human, I was stunned.[26]

Beware of Outsourcing

To reduce costs and improve profits, many jobs in technology, manufacturing, and service are being outsourced to countries such as India, China, and Taiwan, where well-educated, English-speaking workers are being used to do these jobs. For example, programmers in India can produce software at only 10 percent of the cost of these services in the United States. Jobs that are currently being outsourced include accounting, payroll clerks, customer service, data entry, assembly line workers, industrial and production engineers, machine operators, computer-assisted design (CAD) technicians, purchasing managers, textile workers, software developers, and technical support. It is a good idea to consider this trend in choosing your future career and major. Jobs that are most likely to be outsourced are: [27]

- Repetitive jobs, such as accounting,
- Well-defined jobs, such as customer service,
- Small manageable projects, such as software development,
- Jobs in which proximity to the customer is not important, such as technical support.

Jobs that are least likely to be outsourced include:

- Jobs with ambiguity, such as top management jobs,
- Unpredictable jobs, such as troubleshooters,
- Jobs that require understanding of the culture, such as marketing,
- Jobs that require close proximity to the customer, such as auto repair,
- Jobs requiring a high degree of innovation and creativity, such as product design,
- Jobs in entertainment, music, art, and design.

To protect yourself from outsourcing:

- Strive to be the best in the field.
- Be creative and innovative.
- Avoid repetitive jobs that do not require proximity to the customer.
- Choose a career where the demand is so high that it won't matter if some are outsourced.
- Consider a job in the skilled trades; carpenters, plumbers, electricians, hair stylists, construction workers, auto mechanics, and dental hygienists will always be in demand.

New Advances in Biology

Future historians may describe the 21st century as the biology century because of all the developments in this area. If you are interested in biology, it can lead to good careers in the future. One of the most important developments is the Human Genome Project, which has identified the genes in human DNA, the carrier of genetic material. The research done on the human genome has been an impetus for development in some new careers in biotechnology and biomedical technology. Watch the news for future developments that will affect how we all live and work.

Biotechnology will become increasingly important as a way to combat disease, develop new surgical procedures and devices, increase food production, reduce pollution, improve recycling, and provide new tools for law enforcement. Biotechnology includes genomic profiling, biomedical engineering, new pharmaceuticals, genetic engineering, and DNA identification. One of the most promising outcomes of biotechnology will be the production of new pharmaceuticals. About 90 percent of all drugs ever invented have been developed since 1975, and about 6,000 new drugs are waiting for regulatory approval.[28] In the future, biotechnology may be used to find cures for diabetes, arthritis, Alzheimer's disease, and heart disease.

The field of biomedical engineering, which involves developing and testing health care innovations, is expected to grow by 72 percent by 2018.[29] Biomedical technology is the field in which bionic implants are being developed for the human body. Scientists are working on the development of artificial limbs and organs including eyes, ears, hearts, and kidneys. A promising new development in this field is brain and computer interfaces. Scientists recently implanted a computer chip into the brain of a quadriplegic, enabling him to control a computer and television with his mind.[30] Biotechnology also develops new diagnostic test equipment and surgical tools.

Increase in Entrepreneurship

An important trend for the new millennium is the increase in entrepreneurship, which means starting your own business. For the Baby Boom Generation, it was expected that one would have a job for life. Because of rapid changes in society and the world of work, Millennials can expect to have as many as 10 different jobs over a lifetime.[31] A growing number of entrepreneurs operate their small businesses from home, taking advantage of telecommuting and the Internet to communicate with customers. While being an entrepreneur has some risks involved, there are many benefits, such as flexible scheduling, being your own boss, taking charge of your own destiny, and greater potential for future income if your company is successful. You won't have to worry about being outsourced, either.

The Effect of Terrorism and Need for Security

Fear of terrorism has changed attitudes that will affect career trends for years to come. Terrorist attacks have created an atmosphere of uncertainty that has had a negative effect on the economy and has increased unemployment. For example, the airline industry is struggling financially as people hesitate to fly to their vacation destinations. People are choosing to stay in the safety of their homes, offices, cars, and gated communities. Since people are spending more time at home, they spend more money making their homes comfortable. Faith Popcorn, who is famous for predicting future trends, has called this phenomenon "cocooning," which is "our desire to build ourselves strong and cozy nests where we can retreat from the world, enjoying ourselves in safety and comfort."[32] As a result, construction, home remodeling, and sales of entertainment systems are increasing.

Another result of terrorism is the shift toward occupations that provide value to society and in which people can search for personal satisfaction.[33] More people volunteer their time to help others, and are considering careers in education, social work, and medical occupations. When people are forced to relocate because of unemployment, they are considering moving to smaller towns that have a sense of community and a feeling of safety.

As the world population continues to grow, there is continued conflict over resources and ideologies and an increased need for security and safety. Law enforcement, intelligence, forensics, international relations, foreign affairs, and security administration careers will be in demand.

Nontraditional Workers

Unlike traditional workers, nontraditional workers do not have full-time, year-round jobs with health and retirement benefits. Employers are moving toward using nontraditional workers, including multiple job holders, contingent and part-time workers, independent contractors, and temporary workers. Nearly four out of five employers use nontraditional workers to help them become more efficient, prevent layoffs, and access workers with special skills. There are advantages and disadvantages to this arrangement. Nontraditional workers have no benefits and risk unemployment. However, this arrangement can provide workers with a flexible work schedule in which they work during some periods and pursue other interests or gain new skills when not working.

Journal
Entry

Do a quick review of the career trends presented in this chapter:

2

- Moving from the production of goods to service and technology

- Increased opportunities in health care occupations

- Increased need for education

- New green careers

- Increasing diversity in the workplace

- Increased e-commerce and entrepreneurship

- New developments in technology, communication, and biology

- The effect of terrorism and the need for security

- Nontraditional workers

Write one paragraph about how any of these trends might affect your future.

Top Jobs for the Future[34]

Based on current career trends, here are some jobs that should be in high demand for the next 10 years.

Field of Employment	Job Titles
Business	Marketing Manager, Security and Financial Service, Internet Marketing Specialist, Advertising Executive, Buyer, Sales Person, Real Estate Agent, Business Development Manager, Marketing Researcher, Recruiter
Education	Teacher, Teacher's Aide, Adult Education Instructor, Math and Science Teacher
Entertainment	Dancer, Producer, Director, Actor, Content Creator, Musician, Artist, Commercial Artist, Writer, Technical Writer, Newspaper Reporter, News Anchor Person
Health	Emergency Medical Technician, Surgeon, Chiropractor, Dental Hygienist, Registered Nurse, Medical Assistant, Therapist, Respiratory Therapist, Home Health Aide, Primary Care Physician, Medical Lab Technician, Radiology Technician, Physical Therapist, Dental Assistant, Nurse's Aide
Information Technology	Computer Systems Analyst, Computer Engineer, Web Specialist, Network Support Technician, Java Programmer, Information Technology Manager, Web Developer, Database Administrator, Network Engineer
Law/Law Enforcement	Correction Officer, Law Officer, Anti-Terrorist Specialist, Security Guard, Tax/Estate Attorney, Intellectual Property Attorney
Services	Veterinarian, Social Worker, Hair Stylist, Telephone Repair Technician, Aircraft Mechanic, Guidance Counselor, Occupational Therapist, Child Care Assistant, Baker, Landscape Architect, Pest Controller, Chef, Caterer, Food Server
Sports	Athlete, Coach, Umpire, Physical Trainer
Technology	Electrical Engineer, Biological Scientist, Electronic Technician, CAD Operator, Product Designer, Sales Engineer, Applications Engineer, Product Marketing Engineer, Technical Support Manager, Product Development Manager
Trades	Carpenter, Plumber, Electrician
Travel/Transportation	Package Delivery Person, Flight Attendant, Hotel/Restaurant Manager, Taxi Driver, Chauffeur, Driver

Quiz

Career Trends of the Future

Test what you have learned by selecting the correct answers to the following questions:

1. Students in Generation Z are
   a. more optimistic about the future.
   b. fewer in number than previous generations.
   c. increasingly diverse.

2. Use of the Internet will result in
   a. increased e-commerce.
   b. increased use of conventional stores.
   c. decreased mail delivery.

3. The largest group of workers in the United States is in
   a. manufacturing.
   b. information technology.
   c. agriculture.

4. Jobs unlikely to be outsourced include
   a. jobs that require close proximity to the customer.
   b. computer programming jobs.
   c. customer service jobs.

5. Future historians will describe the 21st century as the
   a. art and entertainment century.
   b. biology century.
   c. industrial development century.

How did you do on the quiz? Check your answers: 1. c, 2. a, 3. b, 4. a, 5. b

Work Skills for the 21st Century

Because of rapid changes in technology, college students of today may be preparing for jobs that do not exist right now. After graduation, many college students find employment that is not even related to their college majors. One researcher found that 48 percent of college graduates find employment in fields not related to their college majors.[35] More important than one's college major are the general skills learned in college that prepare students for the future.

To define skills needed in the future workplace, the U.S. Secretary of Labor created the Secretary's Commission on Achieving Necessary Skills (SCANS). Based on interviews with employers and educators, the members of the commission outlined foundation skills and workplace competencies needed to succeed in the workplace in the 21st century.[36] The following skills apply to all occupations in all fields and will help you to become a successful employee, regardless of your major. As you read through these skills, think about your competency in these areas.

Foundation Skills

Basic Skills

- Reading
- Writing
- Basic arithmetic
- Higher-level mathematics
- Listening
- Speaking

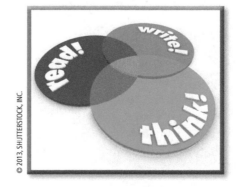

© 2013, SHUTTERSTOCK, INC.

Thinking Skills

- Creative thinking
- Decision making
- Problem solving
- Mental visualization
- Knowing how to learn
- Reasoning

Personal Qualities

- Responsibility
- Self-esteem
- Sociability
- Self-management
- Integrity/honesty

© 2013, SHUTTERSTOCK, INC.

Workplace Competencies

Resources

- **Time.** Selects relevant goals, sets priorities, and follows schedules.
- **Money.** Uses budgets, keeps records, and makes adjustments.
- **Materials and facilities.** Acquires, stores, and distributes materials, supplies, parts, equipment, space, or final products.
- **Human resources.** Assesses knowledge and skills, distributes work, evaluates performance, and provides feedback.

Interpersonal

- **Participates as a member of a team.** Works cooperatively with others and contributes to group efforts.
- **Teaches others.** Helps others learn needed skills.
- **Serves clients/customers.** Works and communicates with clients and customers to satisfy their expectations.
- **Exercises leadership.** Communicates, encourages, persuades, and convinces others; responsibly challenges procedures, policies, or authority.
- **Negotiates to arrive at a decision.** Works toward an agreement involving resources or diverging interests.
- **Works with cultural diversity.** Works well with men and women and with people from a variety of ethnic, social, or educational backgrounds.

Information

- **Acquires and evaluates information.** Identifies the need for information, obtains information, and evaluates it.
- **Organizes and maintains information.** Organizes, processes, and maintains written or computerized records.
- **Uses computers to process information.** Employs computers to acquire, organize, analyze, and communicate information.

Systems

- **Understands systems.** Knows how social, organizational, and technological systems work and operates efficiently within them.
- **Monitors and corrects performance.** Distinguishes trends, predicts impacts of actions on systems operations, and takes action to correct performance.
- **Improves and designs systems.** Develops new systems to improve products or services.

Technology

- **Selects technology.** Judges which procedures, tools, or machines, including computers, will produce the desired results.
- **Applies technology to tasks.** Understands the proper procedures for using machines and computers.
- **Maintains and troubleshoots technology.** Prevents, identifies, or solves problems with machines, computers, and other technologies.

Because the workplace is changing, these skills may be more important than the background acquired through a college major. Work to develop these skills and you will be prepared for whatever lies ahead.

Journal
Entry

Employees need to have strong basic skills to keep up with changes in the workplace. These skills include reading, writing, basic arithmetic, higher level mathematics, listening, and speaking. Comment on your skills in each of these areas. Are there any that you need to improve?

3

How to Research Your Career

After you have assessed your personality, interests, values, and talents, the next step is to learn about the world of work. If you can match your interests to the world of work, you can find work that is interesting and you can excel in it. To learn about the world of work, you will need to research possible careers. This includes reading career descriptions and investigating career outlooks, salaries, and educational requirements.

"The supreme accomplishment is to blur the line between work and play."
ARNOLD TOYNBEE

Career Descriptions

The career description tells you about the nature of the work, working conditions, employment, training, qualifications, advancement, job outlook, earnings, and related occupations. The two best sources of job descriptions are the *Occupational Outlook Handbook* and *Occupational Outlook Quarterly*. The *Handbook*, published by the Bureau of Labor Statistics, is like an encyclopedia of careers. You can search alphabetically by career or by career cluster.

The *Occupational Outlook Quarterly* is a periodical with up-to-date articles on new and emerging occupations, training opportunities, salary trends, and new studies from the Bureau of Labor Statistics. You can find these resources in a public or school library, at a college career center, or on the *College Success Website* at http://www.college success1.com/Links9Career.htm.

"Starting out to make money is the greatest mistake in life. Do what you feel you have a flair for doing, and if you are good enough at it, the money will come."
GREER GARSON

Career Outlook

It is especially important to know about the career outlook of an occupation you are considering. Career outlook includes salary and availability of employment. How much does the occupation pay? Will the occupation exist in the future, and will there be employment opportunities? Of course, you will want to prepare yourself for careers that pay well and have future employment opportunities.

You can find information about career outlooks in the sources listed above, current periodicals, and materials from the Bureau of Labor Statistics. The following table, for example, lists the fastest-growing occupations, occupations with the highest salaries, and occupations with the largest job growth. Information from the Bureau of Labor Statistics is also available online.

Employment Projections 2008–2018[37]

10 Fastest-Growing Occupations	10 Industries with the Largest Wage and Salary Employment Growth	10 Occupations with the Largest Numerical Job Growth
Biomedical engineers	Management, scientific, technical	Registered nurses
Network systems and data communications analysts	Physicians	Home health aides
Home health aides	Computer systems design and related	Customer service representatives
Personal and home care aides	General merchandise stores	Food preparation workers
Financial examiners	Employment services	Personal and home care aides
Medical scientists	Local government	Retail salespersons
Physician assistants	Home health care services	Office clerks
Skin care specialists	Services for elderly and disabled	Accountants and auditors
Biochemists and biophysicists	Nursing care facilities	Nursing aides, orderlies
Athletic trainers	Full-service restaurants	Postsecondary teachers

ZITS © 2009 ZITS PARTNERSHIP, KING FEATURES SYNDICATE

Journal Entry

Go to the *Occupational Outlook Handbook* at http://www.bls.gov/ooh/. Choose one career and write a one-sentence description of the career, list the median salary, and report on the job outlook.

4

Planning Your Education

Once you have assessed your personal characteristics and researched your career options, it is important to plan your education. If you have a plan, you will be able to finish your education more quickly and avoid taking unnecessary classes. You can begin work on your educational plan by following the steps below. After you have done some work on your plan, visit your college counselor or advisor to make sure that your plan is appropriate.

"Think not of yourself as the architect of your career but as the sculptor. Expect to have a lot of hard hammering, chiseling, scraping and polishing."

B.C. FORBES

Activity

Steps in Planning Your Education

_____ 1. **Take your college entrance or assessment tests before you apply to colleges.** Most colleges require the Scholastic Aptitude Test (SAT) or their own local placement tests in order for you to be admitted. You can find information about these tests at your high school or college counseling center or online at http://www.ets.org/ or http://cbweb1.collegeboard.org/index.html. If you are attending a community college, check the college website, admissions office, or counseling office to see what placement exams are required.

_____ 2. **Take English the first semester, and continue each semester until your English requirement is complete.** English courses provide the foundation for further college study. Your SAT or college placement test will determine what level of English you need to take. As a general rule, community colleges require one semester of college-level English. Four-year colleges and universities generally require two semesters or three quarters of college-level English. If your placement scores are low, you may be required to take review courses first.

_____ 3. **Start your math classes early, preferably in the first semester or quarter.** Many high-paying careers require a long series of math classes, particularly those in the sciences, engineering, and business. If you delay taking math courses until later, you may limit your career options and extend your time in college.

_____ 4. **Take the required general education courses.** Find out what your college requires for general education and put these classes on your plan. You will find this information in the college catalog. Be careful to select the correct general education plan. At community colleges, there are different plans for transfer and associate's degree students. At a university, there may be different plans for different colleges within the university. Check with a college counselor or advisor to make sure you have the correct plan.

_____ 5. **Prepare for your major.** Consult your college catalog to see what courses are required for your major. If you are undecided on a major, take the general education courses and start working on a decision about your major. If you are interested in the sciences or engineering, start work on math in the first semester. Start on your major requirements as soon as possible so that you do not delay your graduation.

_____ 6. **Check prerequisites.** A prerequisite is a course that is required before taking a higher-level course. The college catalog lists courses offered and includes prerequisites. Most colleges will not let you register for a course for which you do not have the prerequisite. It is also difficult to succeed in an advanced course without taking the prerequisite first.

_____ 7. **Make an educational plan.** The educational plan includes all the courses you will need to graduate. Again, use the college catalog as your guide.

_____ 8. **Check your plan.** See your college counselor or advisor to check your plan. He or she can save you from taking classes that you do not need and help you to graduate in the minimum amount of time.

Making Good Decisions

Knowing how to make a good decision about your career and important life events is very important to your future, as this short poem by J. Wooden sums up:

There is a choice you have to make,
In everything you do.
And you must always keep in mind,
The choice you make, makes you.[38]

Sometimes people end up in a career because they simply seized an opportunity for employment. A good job becomes available and they happen to be in the right place at the right time. Sometimes people end up in a career because it is familiar to them, because it is a job held by a member of the family or a friend in the community. Sometimes people end up in a career because of economic necessity. The job pays well and they need the money. These careers are the result of chance circumstances. Sometimes they turn out well, and sometimes they turn out miserably.

Whether you are male or female, married or single, you will spend a great deal of your life working. By doing some careful thinking and planning about your career, you can improve your chances of success and happiness. Use the following steps to do some careful decision making about your career. Although you are the person who needs to make the decision about a career, you can get help from your college career center or your college counselor or advisor.

Steps in Making a Career Decision

1. Begin with self-assessment.
   - What is your personality type?
   - What are your interests?
   - What are your talents, gifts, and strengths?
   - What are your values?
   - What lifestyle do you prefer?

2. Explore your options.
   - What careers match your personal characteristics?

3. Research your career options.
   - Read the job description.
   - Investigate the career outlook.
   - What is the salary?
   - What training and education is required?
   - Speak with an advisor, counselor, or person involved in the career that interests you.
   - Choose a career or general career area that matches your personal characteristics.

4. Plan your education to match your career goal.
   - Try out courses in your area of interest.
   - Start your general education if you need more time to decide on a major.
   - Try an internship or part-time job in your area of interest.

5. **Make a commitment to take action and follow through with your plan.**

6. **Evaluate.**
   • Do you like the courses you are taking?
   • Are you doing well in the courses?
   • Continue research if necessary.

7. **Refine your plan.**
   • Make your plan more specific to aim for a particular career.
   • Select the college major that is best for you.

8. **Change your plan if it is not working.**
   • Go back to the self-assessment step.

> "Find a job you like and add five days to every week."
>
> H. JACKSON BROWNE

The Decision-Making Process

• **Dependent decisions.** Different kinds of decisions are appropriate in different situations. When you make a dependent decision, you depend on someone else to make the decision for you. The dependent decision was probably the first kind of decision that you ever made. When your parents told you what to do as a child, you were making a dependent decision. As an adult, you make a dependent decision when your doctor tells you what medication to take for an illness or when your stockbroker tells you what stock you should purchase. Dependent decisions are easy to make and require little thought. Making a dependent decision saves time and energy.

  The dependent decision, however, has some disadvantages. You may not like the outcome of the decision. The medication that your doctor prescribes may have unpleasant side effects. The stock that you purchased may go down in value. When students ask a counselor to recommend a major or a career, they are making a dependent decision. When the decision does not work, they blame the counselor. Even if the dependent decision does have good results, you may become dependent on others to continue making decisions for you. Dependent decisions do work in certain situations, but they do not give you as much control over your own life.

• **Intuitive decisions.** Intuitive decisions are based on intuition or a gut feeling about what is the best course of action. Intuitive decisions can be made quickly and are useful in dealing with emergencies. If I see a car heading on a collision path toward me, I have to swerve quickly to the right or left. I do not have time to ask someone else what to do or think much about the alternatives. Another example of an intuitive decision is in gambling. If I am trying to decide whether to bet a dollar on red or black, I rely on my gut feeling to make a choice. Intuitive decisions may work out or they may not. You could make a mistake and swerve the wrong way as the car approaches or you could lose your money in gambling.

• **Planful decisions.** For important decisions, it is advantageous to use what is called a planful decision. The planful decision is made after carefully weighing the consequences and the pros and cons of the different alternatives. The planful decision-making strategy is particularly useful for such decisions as:
   • What will be my major?
   • What career should I choose?
   • Whom should I marry?

> **Types of Decisions**
> • Dependent
> • Intuitive
> • Planful

The steps in a planful decision-making process:

1. **State the problem.** When we become aware of a problem, the first step is to state the problem in the simplest way possible. Just stating the problem will help you to clarify the issues.

2. **Consider your values.** What is important to you? What are your hopes and dreams? By keeping your values in mind, you are more likely to make a decision that will make you happy.

3. **What are your talents?** What special skills do you have? How can you make a decision that utilizes these skills?

4. **Gather information.** What information can you find that would be helpful in solving the problem? Look for ideas. Ask other people. Do some research. Gathering information can give you insight into alternatives or possible solutions to the problem.

5. **Generate alternatives.** Based on the information you have gathered, identify some possible solutions to the problem.

6. **Evaluate the pros and cons of each alternative.** List the alternatives and think about the pros and cons of each one. In thinking about the pros and cons, consider your values and talents as well as your future goals.

7. **Select the best alternative.** Choose the alternative that is the best match for your values and helps you to achieve your goals.

8. **Take action.** You put your decision into practice when you take some action on it. Get started!

> "When written in Chinese, the word 'crisis' is composed of two characters; one represents danger and the other represents opportunity."
>
> JOHN F. KENNEDY

Quiz

1. When you research the career outlook, you find information about
   a. whether the job is done inside or outside.
   b. the job description.
   c. the salary and availability of employment.

2. In planning your education, it is best to
   a. take English and math early.
   b. try out different courses to find out what you like.
   c. arrange a convenient schedule.

3. Because of rapid changes in technology and the job market, it is important to
   a. major in a science field.
   b. major in a health field.
   c. have good skills in reading, math, communication, and critical thinking.

4. If you make a decision based on your "gut feeling," you risk
   a. making a mistake.
   b. making a dependent decision.
   c. making a planned decision.

5. Career decision making includes
   a. waiting until you finish college to begin the process.
   b. sticking to your plan even if it is not working.
   c. researching your career options.

How did you do on the quiz? Check your answers: 1. c, 2. a, 3. c, 4. a, 5. c

Keys to Success

Life Is a Dangerous Opportunity

Even though we may do our best in planning our career and education, life does not always turn out as planned. Unexpected events happen, putting our life in crisis. The crisis might be loss of employment, divorce, illness, or death of a loved one. How we deal with the crisis events in our lives can have a great impact on our current well-being and the future.

The Chinese word for crisis has two characters: one character represents danger and the other represents opportunity. Every crisis has the danger of loss of something important and the resulting emotions of frustration, sorrow, and grief. But every crisis also has an opportunity. Sometimes it is difficult to see the opportunity because we are overwhelmed by the danger. A crisis, however, can provide an impetus for change and growth. A crisis forces us to look inside ourselves to find capabilities that have always been there, although we did not know it. If life goes too smoothly, there is no motivation to change. If we get too comfortable, we stop growing. There is no testing of our capabilities. We stay in the same patterns.

To find the opportunity in a crisis, focus on what is possible in the situation. Every adversity has the seed of a greater benefit or possibility. Expect things to work out well. Expect success. To deal with negative emotions, consider that feelings are not simply a result of what happens to us, but of our interpretation of events. If we focus on the danger, we cannot see the possibilities.

As a practical application, consider the example of someone who has just lost a job. John had worked as a construction worker for nearly 10 years when he injured his back. His doctor told him that he would no longer be able to do physical labor. John was 30 years old and had two children and large house and truck payments. He was having difficulty finding a job that paid as well as his construction job, and was suffering from many negative emotions resulting from his loss of employment.

John decided that he would have to use his brain rather than his back. As soon as he was up and moving, he started taking some general education courses at the local college. He assessed his skills and identified his strengths. He was a good father and communicated well with his children. He had wanted to go to college, but got married early and started to work in construction instead. John decided that he would really enjoy being a marriage and family counselor. It would mean getting a bachelor's and a master's degree, which would take five or more years.

John began to search for a way to accomplish this new goal. He first tackled the financial problems. He investigated vocational rehabilitation, veteran's benefits, financial aid, and scholarships. He sold his house and his truck. His wife took a part-time job. He worked out a careful budget. He began to work toward his new goal with a high degree of motivation and self-satisfaction. He had found a new opportunity.

© 2013, SHUTTERSTOCK, INC.

Journal

Entry

At times in life, you may face a crisis or setback which causes an unexpected change in plans. If you think positively about the situation, you can think of some new opportunities for the future. This situation is called a dangerous opportunity. Describe a dangerous opportunity you have faced in your life. What were the dangers and what opportunities did you find?

5

> "Life is not about waiting for the storms to pass . . . it's about learning how to dance in the rain."
>
> VIVIAN GREENE

JOURNAL ENTRIES
PLANNING YOUR CAREER AND EDUCATION

Go to http://www.collegesuccess1.com/JournalEntries.htm for Word files of the Journal Entries.

SUCCESS over the Internet

Visit the *College Success Website* at http://www.collegesuccess1.com/

The *College Success Website* is continually updated with new topics and links to the material presented in this chapter. Topics include:

- Future trends
- Planning your major
- Job descriptions
- Career outlooks
- Career information
- Salary
- Interests
- Self-assessment
- Exploring careers
- Hot jobs for the future
- Profiles of successful people
- The personal side of work
- Using the Internet for a job search
- Job openings
- Decision making

Contact your instructor if you have any problems in accessing the *College Success Website.*

Notes

1. Michael T. Robinson, "Top Jobs for the Future," from www.careerplanner.com, 2004.
2. Gail Sheehy, *New Passages* (New York: Random House, 1995), 34.
3. U.S. National Center for Health Statistics, National Vital Statistics Reports (NVSR), *Deaths: Final Data for 2006,* Vol. 57, No. 14, April 17, 2009.
4. Jeff Giles, "Generalization X," *Newsweek,* June 6, 1994.
5. Jane Bryant Quinn, "The Luck of the Xers, Comeback Kids: Young People Will Live Better Than They Think," *Newsweek,* 6 June 1994, 66–67.
6. Ellen Neuborne, http://www.businessweek.com, 1999.
7. Claudia Smith Brison, http://www.thestate.com, 14 July 2002.
8. Neil Howe and William Strauss, *Millennials Rising: The Next Great Generation* (New York: Vintage Books, 2000).
9. *USA Today*, "After Gen X, Millennials, What Should Next Generation Be?", by Bruce Horovitz, May 24, 2012.
10. U.S. Census Bureau, "State and County QuickFacts 2012," http://quickfacts.census.gov/afd/states/00000.html
11. "The first Generation of the Twenty-First Century, an Introduction to the Pluralist Generation" by Magid Generational Strategies, April 30, 2012 from http://magid.com/sites/default/files/pdf/MagidPluralistGenerationWhitepaper.pdf

12. Neuborne, www.businessweek.com, 1999.

13. John Naisbitt, Patricia Aburdeen, and Walter Kiechel III, "How We Will Work in the Year 2000." *Fortune*, 17 May 1993, 41–52.

14. U.S. Bureau of Labor Statistics, *Occupational Outlook Handbook*, 2010–11 Edition, "Overview of the 2008–18 Projections," accessed from http://data.bls.gov

15. Ibid.

16. Ibid.

17. Joyce Lain Kennedy, *Joyce Lain Kennedy's Career Book* (Chicago, IL: VGM Career Horizons, 1993), 32.

18. U.S. Bureau of Labor Statistics, "Overview of the 2008–18 Projections."

19. "U.S. Online Sales to Reach $370 Billion by 2017" by Forrester Research, March 13, 2013 accessed from www.forrester.com

20. Bill Gates, "Microprocessors Upgraded the Way We Live," *USA Today*, 22 June 1999.

21. From "The Microsoft Future According to Bill Gates," accessed from http://www.ameinfo.com/33384.html, 2004.

22. Bill Gates, *Business @ the Speed of Thought: Using a Digital Nervous System* (Warner, 1999). Excerpts available at www.speed-of-thought.com.

23. U.S. Bureau of Labor Statistics, "Overview of the 2008–18 Projections."

24. "Tomorrow's Best Careers," from http://www.future-trends.com, 2004.

25. Dan Tynan, "The Next 25 Years in Tech," www.pcworld.com, January 30, 2008.

26. Anne Foerst, "A New Breed of 'Replicants' Is Redefining What It Means to Be Human," *Forbes ASAP*, 1999.

27. Michael T. Robinson, "Offshoring of America's Top Jobs," from http://www.careerplanner.com, 2004.

28. "Tomorrow's Best Careers," from http://www.future-trends.com, 2004.

29. U.S. Bureau of Labor Statistics, "Overview of the 2008–18 Projections."

30. Roxanne Khamsi, "Paralyzed Man Sends E-Mail by Thought," *News @ Nature.Com*, October 13, 2004.

31. Judith Kautz, "Entrepreneurship Beyond 2000," from www.smallbusinessnotes.com, 2004.

32. Faith Popcorn and Lys Marigold, *Clicking: 16 Trends to Future Fit Your Life, Your Work, and Your Business* (New York: HarperCollins, 1996).

33. James E. Challenger, "Career Pros: Terrorism's Legacy," from www.jobjournal.com, 2003.

34. Michael T. Robinson, "Top Jobs for the Future," CareerPlanner.com, 2008.

35. T. J. Grites, "Being 'Undecided' Could Be the Best Decision They Could Make," *School Counselor* 29 (1981): 41–46.

36. Secretary's Commission on Achieving Necessary Skills (SCANS), *Learning a Living: A Blueprint for High Performance* (Washington, DC: U.S. Department of Labor, 1991).

37. U.S. Bureau of Labor Statistics, "Overview of the 2008–18 Projections."

38. Quoted in Rob Gilbert, ed., *Bits and Pieces*, 7 October 1999.

RATE YOUR SKILLS FOR SUCCESS IN THE WORKPLACE

Read each statement relating to skills needed for success in the workplace. Use the following scale to rate your competencies:

5 = Excellent   4 = Very good   3 = Average   2 = Needs improvement   1 = Need to develop

_____ 1. I have good reading skills. I can locate information I need to read and understand and interpret it. I can pick out the main idea and judge the accuracy of the information.

_____ 2. I have good writing skills. I can communicate thoughts, ideas, and information in writing. I know how to edit and revise my writing and use correct spelling, punctuation, and grammar.

_____ 3. I am good at arithmetic. I can perform basic computations using whole numbers and percentages. I can make reasonable estimates without a calculator and can read tables, graphs, and charts.

_____ 4. I am good at mathematics. I can use a variety of mathematical techniques including statistics to predict the occurrence of events.

_____ 5. I am good at speaking. I can organize my ideas and participate in discussions and group presentations. I speak clearly and am a good listener. I ask questions to obtain feedback when needed.

_____ 6. I am a creative thinker. I can come up with new ideas and unusual connections. I can imagine new possibilities and combine ideas in new ways.

_____ 7. I make good decisions. I can specify goals and constraints, generate alternatives, consider risks, and evaluate alternatives.

_____ 8. I am good at solving problems. I can see when a problem exists, identify the reasons for the problem, and devise a plan of action for solving the problem.

_____ 9. I am good at mental visualization. I can see things in my mind's eye. Examples include building a project from a blueprint or imagining the taste of a recipe from reading it.

_____ 10. I know how to learn. I am aware of my learning style and can use learning strategies to obtain new knowledge.

_____ 11. I am good at reasoning. I can use logic to draw conclusions and apply rules and principles to new situations.

_____ 12. I am a responsible person. I work toward accomplishing goals, set high standards, and pay attention to details. I usually accomplish tasks on time.

_____ 13. I have high self-esteem. I believe in my self-worth and maintain a positive view of myself.

_____ 14. I am sociable, understanding, friendly, adaptable, polite, and relate well to others.

_____ 15. I am good at self-management. I know my background, skills, and abilities and set realistic goals for myself. I monitor my progress toward completing my goals and complete them.

_____ 16. I practice integrity and honesty. I recognize when I am faced with a decision that involves ethics and choose ethical behavior.

_____ 17. I am good at managing my time. I set goals, prioritize, and follow schedules to complete tasks on time.

_____ 18. I manage money well. I know how to use and prepare a budget and keep records, making adjustments when necessary.

_____ 19. I can manage material and resources. I can store and distribute materials, supplies, parts, equipment, space, or products.

_____ 20. I can participate as a member of a team. I can work cooperatively with others and contribute to group efforts.

_____ 21. I can teach others. I can help others to learn needed knowledge and skills.

_____ 22. I can exercise leadership. I know how to communicate, encourage, persuade, and motivate individuals.

_____ 23. I am a good negotiator. I can work toward an agreement and resolve divergent interests.

_____ 24. I can work with men and women from a variety of ethnic, social, or educational backgrounds.

_____ 25. I can acquire and evaluate information. I can identify a need for information and find the information I need.

_____ 26. I can organize and maintain information. I can find written or computerized information.

_____ 27. I can use computers to process information.

_____ 28. I have an understanding of social, organizational, and technological systems and can operate effectively in these systems.

_____ 29. I can improve the design of a system to improve the quality of products and services.

_____ 30. I can use machines and computers to accomplish the desired task.

_____ Total

Score your skills for success in the workplace.

150–121 Excellent
120–91 Very good
90–61 Average
Below 60 Need improvement

From the previous list of workplace skills, make a list of five of your strong points. What do you do well?

From the list of workplace skills, make a list of areas you need to improve.

THE PLANFUL DECISION STRATEGY

Read the following scenario describing a college student in a problem situation. Then, answer the questions that follow to practice the planful decision strategy. You may want to do this as a group activity with other students in the class.

Rhonda is an 18-year-old student who is trying to decide on her major. She was a good student in high school, earning a 3.4 grade point average. Her best subjects were English and American history. She struggled with math and science but still earned good grades in these subjects. While in high school, she enjoyed being on the debate team and organizing the African American Club. This club was active in writing letters to the editor and became involved in supporting a local candidate for city council.

Rhonda is considering majoring in political science and has dreams of eventually going to law school. Rhonda likes being politically involved and advocating for different social causes. The highlight of her life in high school was when she organized students to speak to the city council about installing a traffic light in front of the school after a student was killed trying to cross the street. The light was installed during her senior year.

Rhonda's family has always been supportive, and she values her family life and the close relationships in the family. She comes from a middle-income family that is struggling to pay for her college education. Getting a bachelor's degree in political science and going to law school would take seven years and be very expensive. There is no law school in town, so Rhonda would have to move away from home to attend school.

Rhonda's parents have suggested that she consider becoming a nurse and attending the local nursing college. Rhonda could finish a bachelor's degree in nursing in four years and could begin working part-time as a nurse's aide in a short time. A cousin in the family became a nurse and found a job easily and is now earning a good income. The cousin arranged for Rhonda to volunteer this summer at the hospital where she works. Rhonda enjoys helping people at the hospital. Rhonda is trying to decide on her major. What should she do?

1. State the problem.

2. Describe Rhonda's values, hopes, and dreams.

3. What special interests, talents, or aptitudes does she have?

4. What further information would be helpful to Rhonda in making her decision?

5. What are the alternatives and the pros and cons of each?

Alternative 1	
Pros:	Cons:

Alternative 2	
Pros:	Cons:

Alternative 3 (be creative!)	
Pros:	Cons:

6. Only Rhonda can choose what is best for her. If you were Rhonda, what would you do and why? Use a separate piece of paper, if necessary, to write your answer.

Updated Job Search Strategies

6

Learning
OBJECTIVES

Read to answer these key questions:

- How can I increase my chances for employment after graduation?

- What are some tips for writing my resume and cover letter?

- How do I establish my own personal brand for marketing myself online?

- What are some online tools that can help me find a job?

- How can I prepare for the job interview?

- What is an informational interview?

- What are some options for starting my own business?

- How do I set up a job search plan and begin taking action?

While in college, you can increase your chances of obtaining employment after graduation by using Career Services at your college, volunteering, doing internships, and working part time. Get started by writing your resume and cover letter. Establish your personal brand by assessing your personal strengths and using social media to market yourself to potential employers. Learn about some online tools for searching for that ideal job as well as how to be successful on the interview. Alternatively you may want to consider starting your own business. The most important last step is taking action on your job search plan.

Increasing Your Chances for Employment

Using Your College Career Services

Your College Career Services can assist you in your career planning as well as finding employment, internships, and volunteer opportunities while in college and after graduation. Here are some typical career services:

- Career assessment and counseling
- Career fairs
- Career library
- Employment information
- Job postings
- Job search resources
- Majors and related careers
- Resume assistance
- Interview assistance
- Reference service
- Opportunities for volunteering, internships, and work or study abroad

Volunteering

Volunteering not only helps your community, but it can help your job search in many ways:

- Volunteering improves your confidence and self-worth and gives you a sense of accomplishment. It helps you to develop leadership skills.
- You can add contacts to your network. Most people find jobs through personal and professional contacts.
- If you have little job experience, volunteering looks good on your resume.
- You can learn new skills by volunteering.
- Volunteering is a way to try out a career to see if you like it. For example, if you are thinking about becoming a teacher, volunteer at a school to gain some first-hand experience and to see if teaching is really the career for you.
- Learn about job opportunities while volunteering.
- Ask for recommendations or endorsements after you have finished your volunteer position.

To find a volunteer position, start with Career Services at your college. This office often has volunteer positions related to the majors at their college. You can also re-

© 2013 SHUTTERSTOCK, INC.

search volunteer positions online at volunteermatch.com, which matches your interests to positions available in your community.

Internships

The purpose of an internship is to learn job skills and increase your networking possibilities while you are in college. Internships are often low paid or unpaid positions in a company or organization that is in your area of career interest. Some internships can lead to jobs when you finish college or at least look good on your resume. Colleges set up internships with local companies and may even offer you college credit for them. Begin by contacting Career Services at your college. This office often sets up internships to match the majors at the college. You can also use internmatch.com to begin an Internet search, or join LinkedIn and click on Jobs for Students and Recent Graduates to find opportunities in your area. Another possibility is contacting companies matching your interests and asking them if they have any internship possibilities.

A good internship is one in which you have the opportunity to experience hands-on learning and gain knowledge in the field, which can be valuable in your future career. Often interns shadow employees to learn about their jobs. Internships vary in quality, with the least valuable ones having interns doing busy work with little opportunity to learn valuable skills for the future. It is best to start by figuring out the careers you would like to explore and then carefully investigating what you will be doing as an intern to make sure it is worth your time.

Working While in College

About 80 percent of students work while in college and this employment provides many advantages. It can provide needed income and valuable job experience as well as increased social contacts that can be useful in the future. This work looks good on your resume and can be used for future references. It is also a way of limiting debt by reducing the money you have to borrow for college. Research has shown that students who work 10–15 hours a week are more likely to persist and finish their college degrees. Working while in colleges requires time management skills that can be useful in future employment. Having to plan your study time and work can even result in higher grades, since you will have to schedule your study time and will be more focused on getting your school work done.[1]

However, students are often tempted to work more than the recommended amount, which results in increased stress as they try to balance the demands of employment, study, and social life. This is likely to result in longer time for degree completion or may even interfere with attaining a degree. If you find it necessary to work more than the recommended amount, consider going to college part time.

Journal Entry

What are some ways you can increase your chances of employment while in college? Consider volunteering, internships, or work opportunities.

 1

Get Started with a Resume and Cover Letter

"The nearest to perfection that most people come is when filling out an employment application."

SOURCE UNKNOWN

Your resume is important in establishing a good first impression and provides the basic content for job seeking social media sites such as LinkedIn and Facebook. A resume is a snapshot of your education and experience. It is generally one page in length. You will need a resume to apply for scholarships, part-time jobs, or find a position after you graduate. Start with a file of information you can use to create your resume. Keep your resume on file in your computer or on your flash drive so that you can revise it or post it online as needed.

© 2013, SHUTTERSTOCK, INC.

A resume includes the following basic components:

- Contact information: your name, address, telephone number, and email address
- A brief statement of your career objective
- A summary of your education:
  - Names and locations of schools
  - Dates of attendance
  - Diplomas or degrees received

- A summary of your work and/or volunteer experience
- If you have little directly related work experience, a list of courses you have taken that would help the employer understand your skills for employment
- Special skills, honors, awards, or achievements
- References (people who can recommend you for a job or scholarship)

There is no one best way to write a resume, but here are some helpful tips:

- Begin your resume with your contact information. Make sure that your email is professional. Consider creating a new email for job seeking purposes. Your email should include your first and last name.
- In the job history section, include brief statements about job tasks, including what you did to make your company better. It is helpful to look for key words in the job announcement and make sure these key words are in your resume.
- List your present or most recent job first and work back chronologically.
- If you are just graduating from college and have little work experience, put the education section first along with related coursework.
- Keep in mind that the average resume gets read in 10 seconds. Make sure your resume is organized and brief. Bold those ideas that you want to highlight.
- Do not include personal information or photos.
- Carefully proofread your resume to make sure it has no errors. It is a good idea to have someone else review it also.
- Store your resume on your computer so that you can update it regularly and have it available to post online.

It is easy to upload your content to resume templates online. Here are some resume template sites:

Choose your template from a variety of examples and then create or upload your content.
http://www.myperfectresume.com/

This site has 114 templates depending on your experience and career. You can upload your current resume into a suggested template and add their suggested improvements.
http://www.resume-now.com/

Create a resume and set up a resume webpage.
http://www.jobwinningresume.com/

View sample resume templates and create your resume.
http://www.everymanbusiness.com/human-resources/resume-template/

Ask for a letter of reference from your current supervisor at work or someone in a position to recommend you, such as a college professor or community member. Ask the person to address the letter "To Whom It May Concern" so that you can use the letter many times. If the person is on LinkedIn, ask him or her for an endorsement. The person recommending you should comment on your work habits, skills, and personal qualities. If appropriate, offer to write the letter yourself and then the person can edit it or send it as is. This often helps for people who would like to recommend you, but are very busy. If you wait until you graduate to obtain letters of reference, potential recommenders may no longer be there or may not remember who you are. Always ask if you can use a person's name as a reference. When you are applying for a

© 2013, SHUTTERSTOCK, INC.

job and references are requested, phone the persons who have agreed to recommend you and let them know to expect a call.

While most resumes are shared online, if you need a printed copy, print your resume so that it looks professional. Use a good quality white, tan, or gray paper. It is a good idea to take a printed copy of your resume to an interview.

When you respond to job announcements, you may be asked to send a cover letter with your resume attached. Address your letter to a specific person at the company or organization and spell the name correctly. You can call the personnel office to obtain this information. The purpose of the cover letter is to state your interest in the job, highlight your qualifications, and get the employer to read your resume and call you for an interview. The cover letter should be brief and to the point. Include the following items:

- State the job you are interested in and how you heard about the opening.
- Briefly state how your education and experience would be assets to the company.
- Ask for an interview and tell the employer how you can be contacted.
- Attach your resume.
- Your cover letter is the first contact you have with the employer. Make it neat and free from errors. Use spell check and grammar check, read it over again, and have someone else check it for you.

Select templates and view samples of cover letters online at http://www.cover-letter-now.com/

Quiz

Getting Started

1. While attending college, you can gain valuable experience by working, but it is recommended that if you are a full-time student, you work no more than ___ hours per week.
   a. 30–35
   b. 10–15
   c. 5–10

2. A resume is generally _____ page(s) in length.
   a. four
   b. one
   c. two

3. Begin your resume with your
   a. job objective.
   b. educational history.
   c. contact information.

4. To format your resume, use
   a. an online template.
   b. an outline.
   c. bold headings.

5. The cover letter
   a. contains a brief statement of how your qualifications would be an asset to the company.
   b. includes a detailed list of your education and experience.
   c. does not include a request for an interview.

How did you do on the quiz? Check your answers: 1. b, 2. b, 3. c, 4. a, 5. a

Establishing Your Personal Brand Online

Personal branding is the process by which we market ourselves to others. It is an important concept that has been used to sell products and services. Through the use of social media, you can use this concept to market your strengths to potential employers and to find a satisfying career. Throughout this textbook you have been challenged to become more aware of these personal strengths that can be used to create your own personal brand. Here are the steps for establishing your personal brand and marketing yourself:

> "Everyone should find something they love doing. Then work isn't work. It's a part of themselves. Of who they are."
>
> PAUL MCAULEY

Define Your Brand

The first step in marketing yourself is to define your personal brand. What are your passions, goals, and personal strengths and how can they be used in the job market? Review the assessments in this textbook and write a brief description of your personal brand along with a brief job title. A few examples of a personal brand include financial expert, entrepreneur, educator, consultant, engineer, and personal trainer.

Manage Your Online Presence

Most employers do online searches to find employees and to find information on job candidates before the interview. Make sure that your online presence is a professional one that you would want an employer to see. Make sure that your email address is a professional one or consider setting up an account for job seeking. Google your name and see what information a potential employer can find about you. Take a look at your online sites and make sure that the content is appropriate. Some online content may make it difficult to be hired, including:

- Photos or references to drug or alcohol use or abuse.
- Discriminatory comments on race, religion, or gender.
- Negative comments about previous employers.
- Poor communication skills.

When using Facebook, manage your privacy settings so that no one can see your list of friends, since you can be judged by the company you keep and you have no control over what your friends post. To keep your friends private, specify that no one can tag you in a Facebook photo without your authorization. Be careful about what you put on your front page, since it is the most visible page.

Set up a Nameplate Website

Take control of your online presence by setting up a nameplate website that defines who you are and directs potential employers to your media sites. Good sites for setting up this nameplate include about.me and vizify.com. Both of these sites are free and provide samples that can be helpful in setting up your own site. On these sites, you can upload your photo, include your biography, list your education, describe your work experience, and provide links to LinkedIn or Facebook.

© 2013, SHUTTERSTOCK, INC.

Using Online Tools

At the present time, LinkedIn and Facebook are the most common sites used by employers to research job candidates. Invest some of your time setting up accounts at these sites.

LinkedIn

LinkedIn is a directory of professionals and companies used for job searching, networking, and hiring. Many employers use LinkedIn profiles to search for potential employees. This profile is similar to a resume and includes your education and job experience. Make sure that your profile is complete and well written since it represents who you are online. Since recruiting software is used to search through profiles, use key words in your resume that relate to your desired job. Key words include job requirements, experience, software competencies, education, and previous employers. To find key words, take a look at job listings in your area of interest and expertise and include the words in your profile. It is helpful to include recommendations and endorsements that you can request from other contacts on LinkedIn. Personalize your profile by uploading a photo. Use a current photo and dress appropriately for the type of job you are seeking.

LinkedIn is also a job search tool in which you can search for and apply for jobs within the site. The job listings page allows you to search for jobs by location, industry, company, job function, level or position, employer, or key words. The site can also be used for networking. As you link to others, they can refer you to jobs open at their site. Maintaining a large network is job security, because you can use it for job advancement or to find a new job in the future. You can join groups of other professionals in your area of expertise to receive notices about job openings in your area of interest. Use the status update function to let your contacts know that you are looking for a job.

When you find a specific job listing in which you are interested, you will have the option to apply within LinkedIn or you will be directed to the company website where you will need to create an account. The site also provides company profiles to help you to find the job that best matches your qualifications and help you with information useful for interviewing.

Facebook

Facebook is a social network that can be useful in finding a job. The first step in using your Facebook account to find a job is to clean up your profile to make sure that it does not contain any detrimental content. You can delete any questionable material or even use a software package such as Reppler, which scans your profile for embarrassing content and suggests items you might want to remove. The next step is to post a status update to let your friends know that you are looking for a job and to ask if they know about any job openings.

Use Facebook as a marketing tool. Post samples or links to your work online. If you are a photographer, post some of your photos online. If you

© 2013, SHUTTERSTOCK, INC.

are a writer, post links to material you have written. Keep your materials up to date so that prospective employers can see your best and most recent work. If your chosen company has a public Facebook page, you can show your passion, knowledge, and interest for your dream job by participating in discussion boards that can showcase your expertise. You can "like" the company on Facebook and receive news, information, and job openings from them. You can join or create groups on Facebook to discuss your area of interest. In this way, you may be considered for a job before it is posted.

Use Facebook's Marketplace app to search for jobs. Just click on Jobs in Marketplace and enter the job in which you are interested. It contains information about job openings and links to sites with job applications. Facebook also has an app called Social Jobs that allows you to search for jobs.

Journal Entry

What steps can you take to establish or improve your personal brand?

2

> "We do not go to work only to earn an income, but to find meaning in our lives. What we do is a large part of what we are."
>
> ALAN RYAN

Classified Ads

One of the most traditional ways to find a job is by looking at classified ads in your local newspaper. These ads are available in online editions of newspapers and are searchable by date, category, keyword, and location. CareerBuilder.com, one of the leading job search sites, contains classified ads from many local and national newspapers as well as employer websites. You can search this site by key word, date, location, or zip code and create an alert to have matching job openings emailed to you. With the Advanced Search option, you can search jobs by radius of a certain location, required degree, salary range, and type of employment. Use the Career Builder Job Machine to upload your resume and cover letter.

Job Search Engines

The Do What You Are personality assessment and the MI Advantage career assessment are linked to the SimplyHired job search engine (www.simplyhired.com/), which

© 2013, SHUTTERSTOCK, INC.

sorts jobs by location and category. This search engine also contains information on job trends and salaries. There are numerous Internet sites with job listings including:

- www.indeed.com
- www.linkup.com/
- http://us.jobs/

Employment Agencies

An employment agency is a firm hired by the employer to help with finding the right employees for both temporary and permanent jobs. Employers are motivated to use employment agencies because they do the initial screening and interviewing and save the employer time and money. The cost is usually paid by the employer, but it is a good idea to find out up front if there is any cost to you. Generally the agency works on a contingency basis and does not get paid until they find suitable employees for the job listings. Some private employment agencies do charge for finding you a job and the payment can be a percentage of your first year salary.

The employment agency acts as your advocate and looks for jobs for you. The process begins by submitting a resume and having an interview with the employment agency. The agency will help you with your resume and prepare you for the interview.

Using Email to Find a Job

You can use email as a tool for finding a job by letting people in your network know that you are looking for a position. You can also target potential employers and ask about job openings. Here are some ideas for using email in your job search:

- Use a separate email account for your job search. The account name should be professional and include your first and last name. Gmail and Yahoo offer free email accounts.
- Write your email like a business letter with complete sentences, good grammar, and clear writing. Check your message for accuracy.
- It is important to include the position for which you are applying in the subject line.
- Copy and paste your cover letter into the email and attach your resume.
- Include an email signature with your contact information that includes your full name, email address, and phone number.
- You can include a link to your LinkedIn profile or nameplate website, such as about.me.

Journal
Entry

List some tools that you can use to find a job.

3

The Job Interview

Knowing how to be successful in an interview will help you to get the job that you want. Here are some ideas for being prepared and making a good impression.

- **Learn about the job.**   Before the interview, it is important to research both the company and the job. This research will help you in two ways: you will know if the job is really the one you want and you will have information that will help you to succeed at the interview. If you have taken the time to learn about the company before the interview, you will make a good impression and show that you are really interested in the job. Here are some ways that you can find this information:
  - Visit the company website on the Internet and find out about the company mission and services or products provided. You can find many company profiles on LinkedIn and Facebook.
  - Do any of your friends on Facebook or contacts on LinkedIn work for the company? You can ask for their advice on how to apply for a job. Do any of your family, friends, or teachers know someone who works for the company? If so, you can find out valuable information about the company.
  - The personnel office often has informational brochures that describe the employer.
- **Understand the criteria used in an interview.**   The interviewer represents the company and is looking for the best person to fill the job. It is your job to show the interviewer that you will do a good job. Of course you are interested in salary and benefits, but in order to get hired you must first convince the interviewer that you have something to offer the company. Focus on what you can offer the company based on your education and experience and what you have learned about the company. You may be able to obtain information on salary and benefits from the personnel office before the interview.

  Interviewers look for candidates who show the enthusiasm and commitment necessary to do a good job. They are interested in hiring someone who can work as part of a team. Think about your education and experience and be prepared to describe your skills and give examples of how you have been successful on the job. Give a realistic and honest description of your work.
- **Make a good impression.**   Here are some suggestions for making a good impression:
  - Dress appropriately for the interview. Look at how the employees of the company dress and then dress a little better. Of course, your attire will vary with the type of job you are seeking. You will dress differently if you are interviewing for a position as manager of a surf shop or an entry-level job in an engineering firm. Wear a conservative, dark colored or neutral suit for most professional positions. Do not wear too much jewelry and remove excess body piercings (unless you are working at a piercing shop). Cover any tattoos if they are not appropriate for the workplace.
  - Relax during the interview. You can relax by preparing in advance. Research the company so you have some familiarity with it. Visualize yourself in the interview room feeling confident about the interview.
  - When you enter the interview room, smile, introduce yourself, and shake hands with the interviewer. If your hands are cold and clammy, go to the restroom before the interview and run warm water over your hands or rub them together.

Tips for a Successful Job Interview

- Learn about the job
- Understand the criteria used in the interview
- Make a good impression
- Anticipate interview questions
- Send a thank you note

© 2013, SHUTTERSTOCK, INC.

"Was the interview too early for you?"

- Maintain eye contact with the interviewer and sit up straight. Poor posture or leaning back in your chair could be seen as a lack of confidence or interest in the job.

- **Anticipate the interview questions.**   Listen carefully to the interview questions. Ask for clarification of any question you do not understand. Answer the questions concisely and honestly. It helps to anticipate the questions that are likely to be asked and to think about your answers in advance. Generally, be prepared to talk about yourself, your goals, and your reasons for applying for the job. Have a friend ask you the following interview questions and practice answering them. Here are some questions that are typically asked in interviews and some suggestions for answering them:

1. **What can you tell us about yourself?**
   Think about the job requirements and remember that the interviewer is looking for someone who will do a good job for the company. Talk about your education and experience as it relates to the job. You can put in interesting facts about your life and your hobbies, but keep your answers brief. This question is generally an ice breaker that helps the interviewer get a general picture of you and help you relax.

2. **Why do you want this job? Why should I hire you?**
   Think about the research you did on this company and several ways that you could benefit the company. A good answer might be, "I have always been good at technical skills and engineering. I am interested in putting these technical skills into practice in your company." A not-so-good answer would be, "I'm interested in making a lot of money and need health insurance."

3. **Why are you leaving your present job?**
   Instead of saying that the boss was horrible and the working conditions were intolerable (even if this was the case), think of some positive reasons for leaving such as:
   - I am looking for a job that provides challenge and an opportunity for growth.
   - I received my degree and am looking for a job where I can use my education.

- I had a part-time job to help me through school. I have graduated and am looking for a career.
- I moved (or the company downsized or went out of business).

Be careful about discussing problems on your previous job. The interviewers might assume that you were the cause of the problems or that you could not get along with other people.

4. **What are your strengths and weaknesses?**
Think about your strengths in relation to the job requirements and be prepared to talk about them during the interview. When asked about your weaknesses, smile and try to turn them into strengths. For example, if you are an introvert, you might say that you are quiet and like to concentrate on your work, but you make an effort to communicate with others on the job. If you are an extrovert, say that you enjoy talking and working with others, but you are good at time management and get the job done on time. If you are a perfectionist, say that you like to do an excellent job, but you know the importance of meeting deadlines, so you do the best you can in the time available.

5. **Tell us about a difficulty or problem that you solved on the job.**
Think about some problem that you successfully solved on the job and describe how you did it. Focus on what you accomplished. If the problem was one that dealt with other people, do not focus on blaming or complaining. Focus on your desire to work things out and work well with everyone.

6. **Tell us about one of your achievements on the job.**
Give examples of projects you have done on the job that have turned out well and projects that gave you a sense of pride and accomplishment.

7. **What do you like best about your work? What do you like least?**
Think about these questions in advance and use the question about what you like best to highlight your skills for the job. For the question about what you like the least, be honest but express your willingness to do the job that is required.

8. **Are there any questions that you would like to ask?**
Based on your research on the company, think of some specific questions that show your interest in the company. A good question might be, "Tell me about your company's plans for the future." A not-so-good question would be, "How much vacation do I get?"

9. **Write a thank you note.**
Express your interest in the job and thank the interviewer. It makes a good impression and causes the interviewer to think about you again.

Informational Interviewing

The informational interview is an informal conversation useful for finding career information, exploring your career, building your network, or possibly finding future employment. It is not a job interview and the purpose is not to find employment. It is a way to find more personal information about a career you may be considering and to see if you are a good fit for this occupation.

The informational interview differs from the traditional interview in that you are in control and can ask questions about daily job tasks and how they relate to your interests. It is a great way to build your self-confidence and prepare you for an actual job interview. To obtain an informational interview, check your LinkedIn contacts to see if anyone you know is employed in the industry. Ask your friends, family, and em-

---

Tips for Answering Questions

- Research the company
- Anticipate interview questions
- Listen carefully
- Ask for clarification
- Answer concisely and honestly
- Write a thank you note

"All our dreams can come true, if we have the courage to pursue them."
WALT DISNEY

ployers if they can recommend someone for the interview. You can also work with your college Career Services to see if they have contacts for informational interviews. They often have contacts with college alumni who are willing to speak with students. You can visit websites to identify individuals you would like to interview. Most professionals enjoy helping others who have an interest in their field.

Regard the informational interview as a business appointment and dress the way others dress in this occupation. Make a short appointment (generally 15–30 minutes), state that the purpose of the appointment is to gain career information and advice, and show up on time. You can suggest that the person meet you for coffee (and be sure to pay the bill yourself). Be prepared with a list of questions to ask and to take some brief notes on the information. To begin the interview, give a brief 30 second overview of your career goals and reasons for contacting this person. Remember that the focus of the interview is to find career information. It is best not to ask for a job at this time. If there is a job available and you are a good fit for the job, he or she will likely tell you about it.

It is important to thank the interviewee and then follow up a thank you note or email. Ask the person if he or she is on LinkedIn and if you can request a link online. Bring your resume and hand it to the person at the end of the interview. Do not begin the interview with the resume since you want the focus on career information rather than on yourself.

Here is a sample phone call asking for an informational interview:

Hello. My name is _____ and I am a student at _____University. I found your name at your company website. (Or _____ gave me your name and suggested that I contact you.) Although I am not currently looking for a job, I am interested in the field of _____ and would like to learn more about this occupation. Would it be possible to schedule 15–30 minutes of your time to ask a few questions and get your advice on how to enter this field?

© 2013, SHUTTERSTOCK, INC.

Following is a list of potential interview questions that you can use to keep the conversation going. You probably won't have time to ask all these questions, so choose the ones most that are most personally relevant.

1. What is your job title? What other job titles are commonly used for this position?

2. How did you get this position? What was your career path from entry-level to the position you now have?

3. What are your key job responsibilities? What is the typical day like for you?

4. What skills and education are needed for this job?

5. What are the most valuable courses that you took to prepare you for this job?

6. What are employers looking for (skills, education, personal qualities)?

7. What certificates or degrees are required for this job?

8. What kinds of internships or work experiences are desirable? Are internships available?

9. How does a person obtain this type of employment? How is the job advertised? Is the job market competitive? How can I meet the competition?

10. What are some entry-level positions in this company?

11. What important words should I include on my resume or cover letter?

12. What are the opportunities for advancement?

13. What are some personal characteristics that lead to success on this job?

14. What do you find most satisfying about your job?

15. What are the best and worst things about working in this job? What do you like about your job? Dislike?

16. What stresses you out about your job? What is the most difficult part of your job?

17. What are some of the most important challenges facing your industry today? How will it change in the next 10 years?

18. What is the salary range? What is the potential for advancement?

19. If you were still a college student, what would it be helpful to know about your current job and how to find employment in your field?

20. Can you suggest other sources or persons who could be valuable sources of information for me?

Journal Entry

A friend is looking for a job. What advice would you give him or her about the resume and job interview?

Starting Your Own Business

One solution to the problem of limited job opportunities is to start your own business. The New Millennial and Generation Z are more than twice as likely as past generations to start their own businesses. They are inspired by Mark Zuckerberg who founded Facebook while he was a sophomore at Harvard University. This new trend is powered by the opportunities provided by Facebook and other social media and the availability of support and funding for entrepreneurs. Companies such as RoughDraft. vc and the Experiment Fund are some examples of companies providing investment funds for students who start businesses in college. Websites like Kickstarter help you obtain funds from friends, family, and contacts. Many colleges offer business plan competitions with startup money for new businesses.[2]

If you are considering the option of starting your own business, here are some steps you may want to consider:

- Use time management to take advantage of some of the flexible time between classes and studying to make plans for your own business.
- Realize that starting your own business requires motivation, hard work, and focus. You will need discipline to balance going to class, studying, and starting your own business.
- Building on a central theme in this textbook, "find your passion," build your skills and find ways you can make money doing something that you enjoy. You can also research small business ideas for college students on the Internet.[3]
- Find an entry-level job or internship in the area of your interest so that you can see how the industry works. Look around and see how things can be improved or how you can help the company make more money.
- Find other motivated students who want to start a business and work with them as a group.
- Become familiar with social media. Most new businesses started by college students are promoted through Facebook, Twitter, and Instagram.
- Look around for common problems and find solutions. For example, Daniel Vitiello of Texas Tech University had a friend who dropped his iPhone and Daniel was able to fix it. He started an Internet-based iPhone repair business that earned $25,000 a month.[4]
- Take some summer courses in business, marketing, finance, and entrepreneurship.
- Create a business plan with a description, mission, values statement, pricing, financial projections, start-up capital required, and operations timeline.

You can search the Internet for examples of successful student businesses. Here are just a few examples that show how students look for problems and find solutions using their own personal experience:[5]

- Fei Xiao and Anna Sergeeva of the University of Southern California created trueRSVP, which compares the number of people who RSVP to an event to the number who actually attend. This app is useful for event planners.
- Todd Medema of Carnegie Mellon University created AutoRef, which he hopes will make automobile salespersons obsolete. He site has three million cars from 5,000 dealers.
- Brian Silverman of Duke University created Star Toilet Paper, which features ads from local businesses.
- Wesley Zhao of the University of Pennsylvania created FamilyLeaf, a social media site that allows family members to exchange photos.

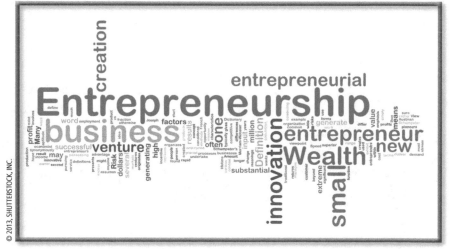

- Gabrielle Palermo of Arizona State University created G3Box to create cost-effective medical clinics out of recycled shipping containers.
- Kenny Nguyen of Louisiana State University observed that his professors needed help in making their lectures better. He founded Big Fish Presentations, which does design, consultation, and production of commercial video.
- Karina Pikhart of the Massachusetts Institute of Technology created 6Dot, a label maker for blind people.
- Jack McDermott of Tufts University used his own experience with speech therapy to create an app, Speech4Good, which helps stutterers improve speech.
- Eric and Matt Lowe of Emerson College are the co-founders of Quiyk, a company that makes athletic apparel for Quidditch, a fictional sport from the Harry Potter novels.

Quiz

Online Resources and Interviewing

1. Personal branding involves
   a. using brand name products.
   b. avoiding name brand products to save money.
   c. using social media to market yourself.

2. One step in managing your online presence is to
   a. limit your use of online tools.
   b. remove inappropriate content.
   c. turn off all privacy controls.

3. At the present time, the most common social media used by employers to research job candidates are
   a. Twitter and Facebook
   b. Tumblr and Instagram
   c. LinkedIn and Facebook

4. The first step in the interview process is
   a. to research information about the company and the job.
   b. ask the interviewer about salary and vacation time.
   c. prepare casual and comfortable clothes.

5. The informational interview is
   a. a good way to find career information and build your network.
   b. a good way to ask for a job.
   c. controlled by the employer.

How did you do on the quiz? Check your answers: 1. c, 2. b, 3. c, 4. a, 5. a

Taking Action

The most important and challenging part of your job search is taking action. Realize that finding a job requires time management and hard work, but it will all pay off when you find a good job. Also realize that you will do many job searches over a lifetime, so keep your resume tuned up, do the best at your current job so that you can get good references, and maintain your professional network.

There will be times when you do not receive a response to a job application, do not get an interview, or do not get the job you consider to be your dream job. It is essential to realize that these are all part of the job search process and to maintain a positive attitude.

Here is a checklist for beginning your job search action plan:

_____ Find out what resources your college Career Services office provides.

_____ Attend job fairs and career conferences.

_____ Assess your skills (multiple intelligences), interests, and personal strengths.

_____ Complete career research on your areas of interest. What are the job activities, skills required, and career outlook?

_____ Investigate opportunities for volunteering and internships.

_____ Identify your goals. Where do you want to be in six months? A year? Five years?

_____ Create your personal brand based on your personal strengths and how they match the job market, including potential job titles.

_____ Set up a Facebook and LinkedIn account if you have not already done so. If you have an existing account check to make sure it is appropriate for a prospective employer to view.

_____ Complete your resume and cover letter.

_____ Do some informational interviews.

_____ Compile reference letters.

_____ Practice interview questions.

_____ Prepare your interview clothes.

_____ Search online career databases for current job openings.

_____ Write thank you letters to anyone helping you in your search.

_____ Use time management. Make a To Do list for each day and set goals for the week and month.

_____ Organize a job search system to keep track of resumes sent, employers contacted, and any other actions taken on your job search. Keep a simple diary that includes these items.

_____ Keep a positive attitude. Stay physically, emotionally, and mentally healthy during your job search.

> "Many of life's failures are people who do not realize how close they were to success when they gave up."
> THOMAS EDISON

As you are conducting your job search, ask these questions to evaluate how you are doing:

• What is working well? What is not working?
• How can I improve?
• What resources are available? Where can I go or who can I ask for help?
• How can I stay motivated?

Journal
Entry

How can you keep yourself motivated during the job search process?

5

Keys to Success

You Are What You Think

"Whether you think you can, or think you can't . . . you're right."

HENRY FORD

Sometimes students enter college with the fear of failure and worry about college success or transitioning to a satisfying career. This belief leads to anxiety and behavior that leads to failure. If you have doubts about your ability to succeed, you might not go to class, attempt the challenging work, or work on your career action plan. It is difficult to make the effort if you cannot see positive results ahead. Unfortunately, failure can lead to a loss of confidence and lack of success in other areas of life as well.

Henry Ford said that "what we believe is true, comes true. What we believe is possible, becomes possible." If you believe that you will succeed, you will be more likely to take actions that lead to your success. Once you have experienced some small part of success, you will have confidence in your abilities and will continue on the road to success. Success leads to more success. It becomes a habit. You will be motivated to make the effort necessary to accomplish your goals. You might even become excited and energized along the way. You will use your gifts and talents to reach your potential and achieve happiness. It all begins with the thoughts you choose.

Watch your thoughts; they become words.
Watch your words; they become actions.
Watch your actions; they become habits.
Watch your habits; they become character.
Watch your character; it becomes your destiny.[6]

Frank Outlaw

To help you choose positive beliefs, picture in your mind how you want your life to be. Imagine it is here now. See all the details and experience the feelings associated with this picture. Pretend it is true until you believe it. Then take action to make your dreams come true.

© 2013, SHUTTERSTOCK, INC.

JOURNALENTRIES

UPDATED JOB SEARCH STRATEGIES

Go to http://www.collegesuccess1.com/JournalEntries.htm for Word files of the Journal Entries.

SUCCESS
over the Internet

Visit the *College Success Website* at http://www.collegesuccess1.com/

The *College Success Website* is continually updated with new topics and links to the material presented in this chapter. Topics include:

- Information about internships and volunteering
- Resume templates
- Sample resumes and cover letters
- Examples of personal brands
- Information on interviewing
- Tips for starting your own business

Contact your instructor if you have any problems in accessing the *College Success Website.*

Notes

1. Kelsey Lucier, "Consider Pros and Cons of Working in College," www.usnews.com, September 13, 2012.
2. Scott Kirsner, "Some Graduates Diving Right into Business," www.bostonglobe.com, April 28, 2013.
3. Felicia Joy, "College Entrepreneurs: 25 Business Ideas That Students Can Launch for $200 or Less," feliciajoyonline.wordpress.com, August 6, 2011.
4. Courtney Rubin, "Create Your Own College Job," www.usnews.com, September 27, 2012.
5. Mariana Simoes and Max Nisen, "16 Great Startups College Students are Working on Right Now," www.businessinsider.com, February 11, 2013.
6. Rob Gilbert, ed., *Bits and Pieces* (Fairfield, NJ: The Economics Press), Vol. R, No. 40, p. 7, copyright 1998.

SAMPLE COVER LETTER

Sara Student
222 College Avenue
San Diego, CA 92019
(619) 123-4567

June 20, 2014

Mr. John Smith
Director of Human Resources
Future Technology Company
111 Technology Way
La Jolla, CA 92111

Dear Mr. Smith:

At our college job fair last week, I enjoyed speaking with you about some new engineering jobs available at Future Technology Company. As you suggested, I am sending my resume. I am interested in your opening for an electrical engineer. Is there anything else I need to do to apply for this position?

While at UCSD, I gained experience in laboratory projects, writing scientific reports, and preparing technical presentations. Some engineering projects that I completed relate to work done at your company:

- Constructed a programmable robot with motor and sensors
- Worked with a group of students on the design of a satellite communications system
- Completed lab projects on innovative fiber-optic fabrication techniques
- Proposed a design for a prosthetic device to help the visually impaired

For my senior design project, I used my knowledge of digital signal processing and systems integration to design and construct a voice modulator. This project involved applying theory to hardware and understanding information processing as well as the relation of a computer to its controlled devices.

I am excited about the possibility of continuing work in this field and would enjoy the opportunity to discuss my qualifications in more detail. I am available for an interview at your convenience. I look forward to hearing from you.

Sincerely,

Sara Student

Encl.: Resume

SAMPLE RESUME FOR A RECENT COLLEGE GRADUATE

Sara Student

222 College Avenue; San Diego, CA 92019

(619) 123-4567

saraengineer@aol.com

OBJECTIVE Electrical Engineer

HIGHLIGHTS Recent degree in Electrical Engineering
Specialized coursework in electromagnetism, photonics and lasers, biomedical imaging devices, and experimental techniques

EDUCATION B.S., Electrical Engineering, University of California, San Diego, CA, 2010
A.S. with Honors, Cuyamaca College, El Cajon, CA, 2008

KEY RELATED COURSES
- **Circuits and systems:** solving network equations, Laplace transforms, practical robotics development
- **Electromagnetism:** Maxwell's equations, wave guides and transmission, electromagnetic properties of circuits and materials
- **Experimental techniques:** built and programmed a voice processor; studied transducers, computer architecture, and interfacing; applied integrated construction techniques
- **Photonics and lasers:** laser stability and design, holography, optical information processing, pattern recognition, electro-optic modulation, fiber optics
- **Biomedical imaging devices:** microscopy, x-rays, and neural imaging; designed an optical prosthesis
- **Quantum physics:** uncertainty principle, wave equation and spin, particle models, scattering theory and radiation

SKILLS **Computer Skills:** PSpice, Matlab, Java, DSP, Assembly Language, Unix, Windows, Microsoft Word, Excel, and PowerPoint
Technical Skills: Microprocessors, circuits, optical components, oscilloscope, function generator, photovoltaics, signal processing, typing, SQUID testing
Personal Skills: Leadership, good people skills, organized, responsible, creative, motivated, hardworking, good writing skills

EMPLOYMENT Intern, Quantum Design, La Jolla, CA, Summer 2013
Computer Lab Assistant, UCSD, La Jolla, CA, 2012–2013
Teacher's Aide, Cuyamaca College, El Cajon, CA, 2010–2012
Volunteer, Habitat for Humanity, Tijuana, Mexico, 2009–2010

INTERESTS Optics, computing, programming, physics, electronic music, sampling, marine biology, and scuba diving

ACHIEVEMENTS Advanced Placement Scholar
Dean's List, Phi Theta Kappa Honor Society
Provost's Honors List

RESUME WORKSHEET FOR YOUR IDEAL CAREER

Use this worksheet to prepare a resume similar to the sample on the previous page. Assume that you have graduated from college and are applying for your ideal career.

1. What is the specific job title of your ideal job?

2. What are two or three qualifications you possess that would especially qualify you for this job? These qualifications can be listed under Highlights on your resume.

3. List your degree or degrees, major, and dates of completion.

4. List five courses you will take to prepare for your ideal career. For each course, list some key components that would catch the interest of your potential employer. Use a college catalog to complete this section.

5. List the skills you would need in each of these areas.

Computer skills:

Technical or other job-related skills:

Personal skills related to your job objective:

6. List employment that would prepare you for your ideal job. Consider internships or part-time employment.

7. What are your interests?

8. What special achievements or awards do you have?

INTERVIEW WORKSHEET

Answer the following questions to prepare for the interview for your ideal job. If you do not know what your ideal job is, pretend that you are interviewing for any professional job. You may want to practice these questions with a classmate.

1. What can you tell us about yourself?

2. Why are you leaving your present job?

3. What are your strengths and weaknesses?

4. Tell us about a difficulty or problem that you solved on the job.

5. Tell us about one of your achievements on the job.

6. What do you like best about your work? What do you like least?

7. Are there any questions that you would like to ask?

POST ASSESSMENT

Now that you have finished the text, complete the following assessment to measure your improvement. Compare your results to the assessment taken at the beginning of the course.

Measure Your Success

The following statements represent major topics included in the textbook. Read the following statements and rate how true they are for you at the present time. After you have finished the assessment, compare your results with the same assessment you took in Chapter 1.

5   Definitely true
4   Mostly true
3   Somewhat true
2   Seldom true
1   Never true

_____ I understand the steps in choosing a major and career.

_____ I understand how education will affect my future earnings.

_____ I know how to use motivation techniques to be successful.

_____ I have control over my life and can create my future.

_____ I usually practice positive thinking.

_____ I have a visual picture of my future success.

_____ I have a clear idea of what happiness means to me.

_____ **Total points for Creating Success**

_____ I can describe my personality type.

_____ I can list careers that match my personality type.

_____ I can describe my personal strengths and talents based on my personality type.

_____ I understand how my personality type affects how I manage my time and money.

_____ I know what college majors are most in demand.

_____ I am confident that I have chosen the best major for myself.

_____ Courses related to my major are interesting and exciting to me.

_____ **Total points for Personality and Major**

_____ I can describe my vocational interests.

_____ I can list careers that match my vocational interests.

_____ I can list my top five values.

_____ I generally consider my most important values when making decisions.

_____ My actions are generally guided by my personal values.

_____ My personal values motivate me to be successful.

_____ I can balance work, study, and leisure activities.

_____ **Total points for Interests and Values**

_____ I understand the concept of multiple intelligences.

_____ I can list my multiple intelligences.

_____ I can list my personal strengths.

_____ I can list the careers that match my personal strengths.

_____ I am aware of my emotional intelligence and use it to create positive relationships.

_____ I have a list of my short-term and long-term goals.

_____ I believe that I can create my own future.

_____ **Total points for Multiple Intelligences and Goal Setting**

_____ I understand how current employment trends will affect my future.

_____ I know what work skills will be most important for the 21st century.

_____ I know how to do career research.

_____ I am aware of the job outlook for careers in which I am interested.

_____ I have an educational plan that matches my academic and career goals.

_____ I know the steps in making a good career decision.

_____ I know how to choose a satisfying career.

_____ **Total points for Career and Education**

_____ I know how to increase my chances for employment while in college.

_____ I know how to write a good resume and cover letter.

_____ I understand personal branding and know how to market myself online.

_____ I know how to use social media to find a job.

_____ I am familiar with online tools for job search.

_____ I know how to interview for a job.

_____ I know about options for creating my own business.

_____ **Total points for Job Search Strategies**

Total Your Points

_____ Creating Success

_____ Personality and Major

_____ Interests and Values

_____ Multiple Intelligences and Goal Setting

_____ Career and Education

_____ Job Search Strategies

_____ **Grand total points**

If you scored

190–210 You have excellent skills for creating your future career, but you can always learn something new.

168–189 You have good skills for creating your future career, but could improve.

126–167 You have average skills for creating your future career, but will increase your skills in this course.

Below 126 Your score is low right now, but this course will help you to increase the skills for creating your future career.

Use these scores to complete the Success Wheel on the following page.

SUCCESS WHEEL

Use your scores from "Measure Your Success" to complete the following success wheel. Use different colored markers to shade in each section of the wheel.

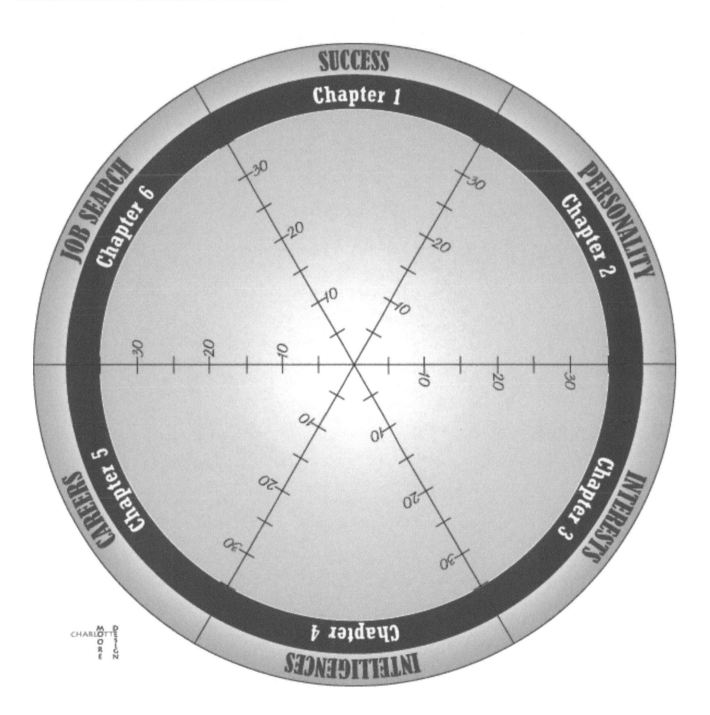

Compare your results to those on this same assessment in Chapter 1. How much did you improve?

COURSE EVALUATION

1. What did you think of this course?

   _____ A. This was one of the best courses I ever had.

   _____ B. This course was excellent.

   _____ C. This course was very good.

   _____ D. This course was satisfactory.

   _____ E. This course was not satisfactory.

2. How helpful was this course in choosing a major or career or confirming you choice of a major or career?

   _____ A. Extremely helpful

   _____ B. Very helpful

   _____ C. Helpful

   _____ D. Not helpful

   _____ E. Unknown

3. How helpful was this course in improving your chances for success in college?

   _____ A. Extremely helpful

   _____ B. Very helpful

   _____ C. Helpful

   _____ D. Not helpful

   _____ E. Unknown

4. How helpful was this course in improving your chances for success in your future career?

   _____ A. Extremely helpful

   _____ B. Very helpful

   _____ C. Helpful

   _____ D. Not helpful

   _____ E. Unknown

5. How helpful was this course in building your self-confidence?

   _____ A. Extremely helpful

   _____ B. Very helpful

   _____ C. Helpful

   _____ D. Not helpful

   _____ E. Unknown

6. Please rate the textbook used for this class.

_____ A. Outstanding

_____ B. Excellent

_____ C. Satisfactory

_____ D. Needs improvement

7. Please rate the instructor in this class.

_____ A. Outstanding

_____ B. Excellent

_____ C. Satisfactory

_____ D. Needs improvement

8. Would you recommend this course to a friend?

_____ A. Yes

_____ B. No

9. Do you plan to continue your college studies next semester?

_____ A. Yes

_____ B. No

10. Please tell what you liked about this class and how it was useful to you.

11. Do you have any suggestions for improving the class or text?

INDEX

A

Acts of kindness, 17–18
Advertisements, classified, 162
Aesthetic needs, 81
Agencies, employment, 163
Artistic interests, 72
Associate degree, earnings, 4

B

Baby boomers, 123–125
Bachelor's degree, earnings, 4
Beliefs, 11–13
Belongingness, 81
Biological needs, 81
Biology, 131–132
Bodily-kinesthetic intelligence, 101
Body care, 19
Business, starting, 168–170

C

Career interests, 72–80
    artistic interests, 72
    conventional interests, 73–80
    enterprising interests, 72–73
    investigative interests, 72
    lifestyle triangle, 80
    realistic interests, 72
    relationships between, 73
    social interests, 72
Careers, 121–151
    choice of, 47–60
    college services, 154
    decisions regarding, 140–141
    descriptions of, 137
    multiple intelligences, 106
    outlook, 138
    researching, 137–138
Classified ads, 162
College career services, 154
College success website, 22, 66, 87, 114,
    144, 173
Communication, 129–130
Competencies, workplace, 136–137
Control of life, 9–13
    locus of control, 9–10
    proactivity, 11
    successful beliefs, 11–13

synergy, 11
    understanding others, 11
    win-win thinking, 11
Conventional interests, 73–80
Criteria for interview, 164
Cultivating optimism, 17

D

Decision-making process, 45–46, 141–151
    thinking, 45
Decisions
    career, 140–141
    dependent, 141
    intuitive, 141
Dependent decisions, 141
Descriptions of career, 137
Diverse workforce, 127–128

E

e-commerce, 128
Earnings
    education and, 3–5
    by education level, 4
Echo boomers, 123
Education, 121–151
    biology, 131–132
    career decision, 140–141
    communication, 129–130
    decision-making process, 141–151
    descriptions of career, 137
    e-commerce, 128
    employment trends, 122–135
    entrepreneurship, 132
    foundation skills, 135
    health care, 126
    increased need for, 126–127
    microprocessor, 128–129
    need for, 126–127
    nontraditional workers, 133
    outsourcing, 130–131
    planning, 139
    planning education, 139
    researching career, 137–138
    security, 132
    technology, 125–126, 129–130
    terrorism, 132
    thinking skills, 136
    work skills, 135–137